The Netherlands in a Nutshell

The Netherlands in a Nutshell

Highlights from Dutch History and Culture

REVISED EDITION 2020

Amsterdam University Press

www.canonvannederland.nl/en

© 2020 Stichting entoen.nu

ISBN 978-94-6372-765-5
NUR 688/840

Translation: Marjan Doets, Eurotext Vertaalbureau
Design: Kok Korpershoek

Contents

Foreword

What basic knowledge of Dutch history and culture should we pass on to future generations of Dutch citizens? This was the difficult question facing the Committee for the Development of the Dutch Canon in 2005, when the minister of Education, Culture and Science asked it to design a canon of the Netherlands.

The commission came up with a creative response: a Canon in fifty key topics, or 'windows', consisting of important people, inventions and events which together show how the Netherlands has developed into the country that it now is. Each Dutch student is supposed to become familiar with these windows in the course of their primary and secondary education.

This Canon was created by bringing together a number of specialists and allowing them to consult for a year with one another and with a selection of interested individuals and stakeholders. A website gave every Dutch citizen the opportunity to voice his or her opinion. The result was a 'Canon van Nederland' that found widespread acceptance and extensive use, particularly in primary education. The Netherlands is one of the very few countries in the world where a 'canon' figures prominently in a school curriculum.

The Dutch historian Pieter Geyl once famously stated that 'history is an argument without end'. The windows approach to the canon encouraged that kind of discussion. Nevertheless it became clear that the canon, which had not significantly changed since 2006, was in need of revision. In 2019, the minister of education assigned this work to a new commission, which completed its work in June of 2020.

This commission replaced ten of the fifty windows with new ones, revised the content of some others, and rewrote all of them to make them more accessible. It added more international references, sought a greater balance in the kinds of windows offered (in respect to gender for instance) and encouraged even more than before a multi-perspectival approach. And it devised seven main motifs by which the windows are connected to one another (see the back of the book for an overview).

One could argue that in both its creation and in its revision, the Canon of the Netherlands was created in a typically Dutch way: it was not decreed by a central authority or a single lofty institution, and neither was it created by a majority vote in a referendum, but by a broad panel of specialists representing the breadth of the Netherlands itself. The way in which this Canon was created may say as much about the Netherlands as do the fifty windows themselves.

In this book, the fifty windows of the revised Canon constitute the Netherlands in a nutshell, to anyone who would like to make a quick acquaintance with this 'low country by the sea'.

On behalf of the committee,
James Kennedy

The Canon of the Netherlands

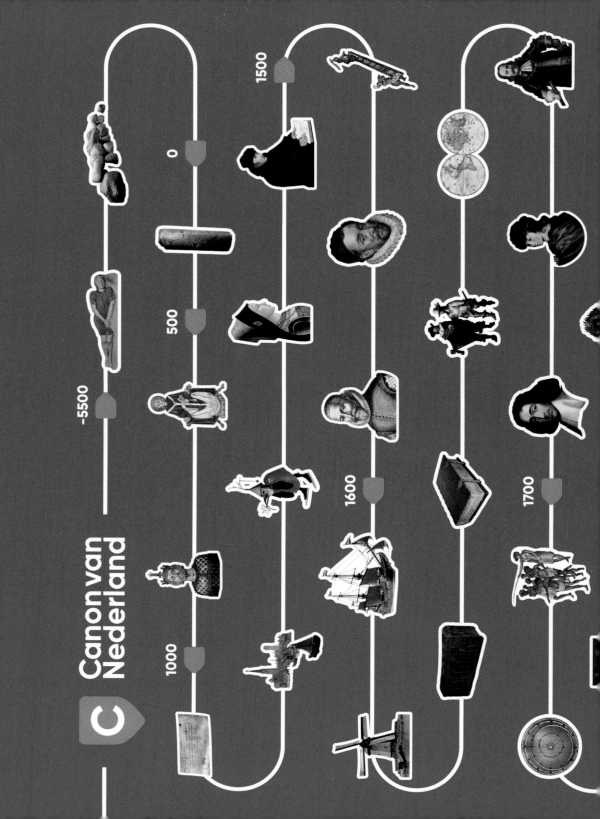

Canon van Nederland

-5500

0

500

1000

1500

1600

1700

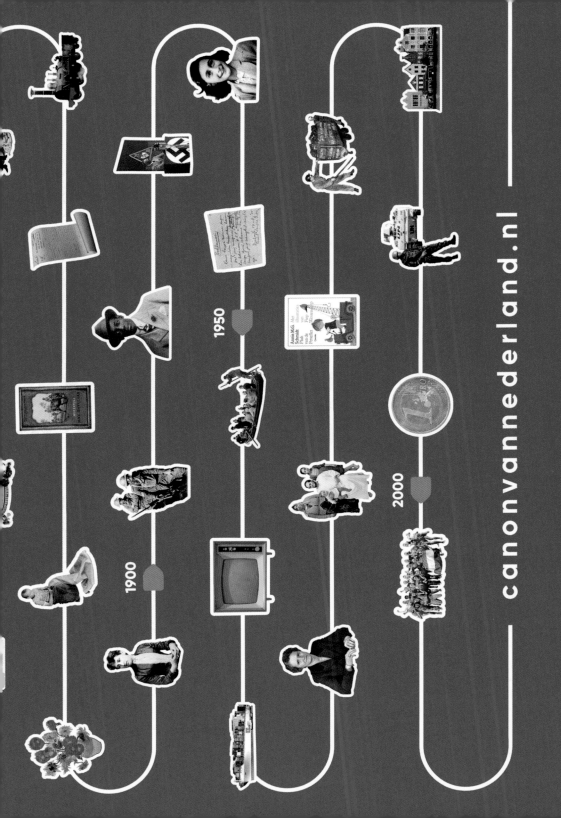

1950

1900

2000

canonvannederland.nl

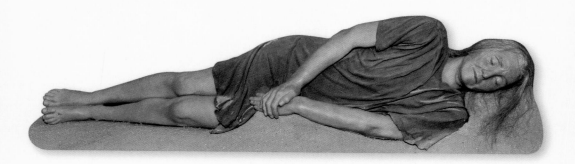

5500 BC

Trijntje

The hunter-gatherers

Rather than staying in the same spot, the first inhabitants of our river country travel from one area to the next. They hunt, fish, and collect fruit, nuts, turnips, and seeds. The winters are spent in permanent camps at dry locations. In 1997, the skeleton of hunter-gatherer Trijntje was dug up at the former site of one of these settlements.

The eldest human skeleton found in the Netherlands belongs to a woman. Some 7,500 years ago, she is lovingly buried in a sand dune in the swampy river area. At the time of her death, she is between forty and sixty years old. She has borne at least one child. When archaeologists excavate the small settlement in which she lived, her skeleton is still complete. This means that her face and body can be reconstructed. Because she is found near a railway track, she is named Trijntje (a traditional Dutch name and a homonym for "little train"). We do not know her actual name, nor do we know which language she used to speak.

Ice ages

Before modern man (Homo Sapiens) arrives in Europe, some 45,000 years ago, it was already inhabited by human species. For example, the Neanderthals, who live in the period we refer to as the old stone age, which commences 300,000 years ago. They live in a vast steppe-like landscape featuring rivers and valleys, with barely any vegetation. The North Sea level is much lower than nowadays and during the coldest periods, it dries up. The Neanderthals live in huts and know how to make fire.

Hunters and gatherers

Trijntje lives much later, in the Middle Stone Age, among a group of some 25 people. Every year, the group travels back and forth between summer and winter camps. They probably live in huts made of branches, reeds, and perhaps animal skins. The hunter-gatherers make sophisticated flint tools, such as scrapers, knives, and arrowheads. Travelling is done on foot and by canoe. To the rhythm of the seasons, they live off what nature offers them, such as edible mammals, fish, and birds.

For the entire winter, Trijntje and her group live on a river dune. They hunt a range of animals such as beavers, otters, seals, aurochs, and a wide array of bird species. Boar and red deer feature most frequently on the menu. Nets and fish traps are used to catch fish, mostly pike. Dogs have evolved into beloved companions; three are buried next to Trijntje.

The group uses all the parts of the animals they catch. The meat is grilled. Tendons and bowels are used to make bows and arrows. Skins and furs are converted into clothing and bags. Bones and antlers are used for all sorts of tools, such as axes and needles. The perforated deer teeth that have been found were perhaps worn as jewellery. We do not know exactly what Trijntje looked like, but DNA tests of skeletons from the Early and Middle Stone Ages have revealed that many people of those times were dark-skinned, with blue eyes. The spread of specific types of flint points to trade, which in some cases covered long distances.

The advent of agriculture

On the timeline of human history, Trijntje and her tribe feature near the end of the period of travelling hunter-gatherers in these regions. Some 7,300 years ago, groups of migrants from the east settle in the hills of Limburg; they live off arable farming and stockbreeding. Food-growing methods spread rapidly. The advent of agriculture marks the beginning of the end of the hunter-gatherer era in these regions, although the two modes of existence continue to be combined for more than two thousand years.

3000 BC

Megalithic tombs

The first farmers

Nobody knows how they did it, but some five thousand years ago,
early farmers managed to move huge, heavy boulders in order to build graves.
These megalithic tombs are the tangible monuments of a peasant people that
left their hunter-gatherer existence behind to settle in permanent locations.

Burial grounds

The megalith builders are not the earliest farmers in the Netherlands: they arrive comparatively late. The first farmers belong to the so-called "linear pottery culture"; they lived some seven thousand years ago in the hills of Limburg. Some two thousand years later, the megalith builders settle in the Netherlands. What little they have left behind is usually buried deep in the ground. However, in the provinces of Drenthe and Groningen, their traces are there for everyone to see. They are megalithic tombs, made of giant stones that were arranged and piled up by human hands. The megalithic structures serve as communal burial grounds.

This type of stone tombs is not uncommon in those days: some 35,000 have been found all over Europe. They are constructed of huge erratic blocks, transported from Scandinavia by glaciers during one of the ice ages, some 150,000 years ago.

Way of life
The megalith builders live in farmhouses made of wood and mud. They use wooden and stone tools, and make clay pottery to store supplies. Such pots are also included in the funerary gifts that are given to the deceased. On account of their shape, archaeologists call such pots "funnel beakers". Artefacts that are found in the soil in and around the megalithic tombs enable us to reconstruct their way of life. However, it is still not quite clear how these people managed to lift boulders weighing up to twenty thousand kilos off the ground. They probably build some sort of earthen ramps and use thin round logs to roll the stones. Once the boulders are in place, the ground underneath is dug away, thus creating a burial chamber.

Inventions
The megalithic tombs tie in with a prolonged period of prehistoric discoveries and inventions, which have had a major impact on the development of Europe. From 3000 BC onwards, metal – gold, copper, and bronze – is being used on a wider scale. Trade networks develop all over Europe in order to obtain metal objects. Groups of migrants from present-day Ukraine and Russia travel to western Europe, taking along inventions such as the wheel and the wagon. And their language, which constitutes the basis for the largest family of languages in the world, the Indo-European languages. This migration wave is still reflected in both the languages that are spoken in Europe and the current DNA of the Dutch and other Europeans.

Monuments
In Drenthe, more than fifty megalithic tombs have been preserved; Groningen has two. Yet there must have been many more. Over the centuries, a great many tombs have disappeared, for instance because the boulders were used as construction material. From the seventeenth century onwards, the value of the megalithic tombs garners more attention. In 1734, this results in a Monument Act, which is intended to prevent the destruction of megalithic tombs.

47 AD – c. 350 AD

The Roman *Limes*

On the frontiers of the Roman world

Two thousand years ago, the northern frontier of the immense Roman Empire runs straight across the current territory of the Netherlands. In Latin, this frontier is referred to as *"limes"*. The *limes* extends for thousands of kilometres in total. It runs from the north of England up to the edge of the Sahara Desert in Africa. In the Low Countries, the frontier is formed by the River Rhine.

Influence

In order to defend their frontier, the Romans build several watchtowers and army camps. In the vicinity of Nijmegen, a camp is established that can accommodate two legions of six thousand soldiers each. With their tunics, shiny helmets, shields, and swords, the well-trained Roman soldiers must have made quite an impression on the local population. The Roman presence certainly exerts a major influence on the environment. Impressive temples and bathing establishments are erected, and farms are created. Increasingly more land is used for agriculture.

16

The Romans also bring the first written language to the region: Latin. They introduce their own idolatry but also incorporate Germanic gods. At several locations, they erect temples devoted to Hercules Magusanus, a combination of a Roman and Germanic deity. Also, trade flourishes, because in addition to its role as a frontier, the River Rhine also serves as a major transport artery. Supplies and commodities are shipped in.

Attack from the north

To Roman eyes, the uncivilised world commences north of the limes. This area is inhabited by Celtic and Germanic tribes. The limes also evolves into a more symbolic border, which sets a limit to the power of Rome. The direct dominion of the Romans does not extend much farther than the River Rhine, although their initial ambition is to expand their territory. This ambition is thwarted in the year 9 AD, when Germanic troops crush three Roman legions near the Teutoburg Forest, in current Germany.

North of the River Rhine, Roman dominion over Frisian territory continues until 28 AD, when the Frisians successfully revolt against the Roman oppressors. At the Emperor's command, in 47 AD the Romans start to retreat behind the River Rhine, which thus becomes the natural northern frontier. After the revolt, trade continues as usual, as does the Roman cultural influence on the Frisians.

Roman territory south of the limes also sees revolts against Roman oppression. The best-known example is the Batavian uprising in 69 AD, led by Julius Civilis. For a long time, the Batavians lived in peace with the Romans and even served in the Roman army. However, during the struggle for power that arose after the death of Emperor Nero, Civilis takes charge of an insurrection that the Romans manage to suppress after about a year. Hundreds of years later, during the Eighty Years' War, the story of this Batavian uprising is used as a source of inspiration for the resistance against Spain.

Traces

From the third century AD, the number of Germanic attacks increases considerably. The Romans are forced to leave the limes and eventually retreat behind the Alps. Traces of the Roman era can still be found in the Netherlands. Several locations in the old frontier region date back to Roman times. Furthermore, new artefacts are regularly found. For example, a watchtower and two vessels were discovered during the construction of the new Leidsche Rijn district in the city of Utrecht.

658-739

Willibrord

The spread of Christianity

Around the year 700, Christians regard the Frisian inhabitants of the coastal region as pagans. These people resist conversion, until the arrival of the English monk Willibrord. He manages to win over many Frisians to the Christian faith, although a proportion of them still continue to hang on to their old faith.

Franks and Frisians

In 690, the English Willibrord arrives in the Low Countries. With twelve companions, this monk and missionary from Northumbria has crossed the North Sea to spread the Christian faith in Frisia. His own country has already been Christianised. The Frisian territory extends from the Westerschelde coastal stretch to the River Weser. The Frisians stick to their old customs and believe in such gods as Wodan and Donar.

His predecessors have informed Willibrord that converting the Frisians is no easy matter. For that reason, Willibrord seeks support from the Frankish Court. The Frisian territory borders the Frankish Empire that has already adopted the Christian faith two centuries earlier, under the reign of King Clovis. The Frisian nobility regards the missionaries as accomplices to the Franks, with whom the Frisians regularly clash.

The tension between Franks and Frisians features a history of alternate alliances and conflicts. The border between Frisian and Frankish territories is not clearly defined: after each conflict, either the Frisians move a short distance south or the Franks move up north. Utrecht thus falls under alternate rule. Around 630 – during a period of Frankish successes – King Dagobert of the Franks commissions Utrecht's first church on the current Dom Square. Shortly afterwards, it is destroyed under Frisian rule.

Christianisation

The Frankish monarchs urge the Pope to appoint Willibrord "Archbishop of the Frisians". This enables the Franks to exert influence, via the Archbishop, over the administration of the Frisian territories. In 696, Willibrord settles in Utrecht and rebuilds the destroyed church. He also commissions the construction of a new church and founds a monastery.

From Utrecht, the missionaries subsequently spread across the lands of the Frisians. Their efforts bear some fruit: by the end of Willibrord's life – he dies in 739 – many people in the coastal region have converted to Christianity. In the rest of the Frisian territory, however, the missionaries encounter opposition. All Dutch school children know the story of Boniface, who goes on a mission to Dokkum and is murdered around 754. Not until the end of the eighth century do Frankish weapons finally end the conflict. Subsequently, the Christianisation of Europe gradually spreads to the northeast. It is a long process. In Scandinavia, Christianisation starts in 1100. Europe's last "pagan" nation, Lithuania, converts to Christianity in 1387.

Baptismal vows

Every convert must say baptismal vows. One such document from Willibrord's time survives, written in the Dutch of 1400 years ago. It states the Germanic habits and customs the converts must break with. The vows read:

> *"Ec forsacho diabolae, end allum diobolgeldae, end ec forsacho allum dioboles wercum and wordum, Thunaer ende Woden ende Saxnote ende allum them unholdum the hira genotas, sint. Ec gelobo in Got alamehtigan fadaer. Ec gelobo in Crist gotes suno. Ec gelobo in Halogan Gast."*

> "I forsake the Devil and all the Devil's sacrifices, and I forsake all the works and words of the Devil, Donar, Wodan, Saxnot, and their attendant idols. I believe in God the Almighty Father, in Christ God's Son, and in the Holy Spirit."

747?-814

Charlemagne

Emperor of the West

Charlemagne is one of the greatest rulers of the early Middle Ages.
By continuously waging war, he manages to subjugate a large part of western
Europe by 800, encompassing what is now the Netherlands. Named Charles,
he is dubbed Charles le Magne [Charles the Great] because of his vast empire.
Moreover, at a height of 1.84 m (6 ft), he was impressively tall for his time.

War

In 768 – following the deaths of his father and his brother – Charles is crowned King of the Franks. Throughout his reign, Charles wages war: against the Islamic rulers of the Iberian Peninsula (the current Spain and Portugal), against the Lombards in the south (the current Italy), and against the Danes and the Saxons in northwest Europe. Occasionally, his troops resort to brute force and mass executions. His many campaigns enable Charles to expand his empire increasingly further and eventually, the Frankish Empire covers large parts of Europe. In the year 800, Pope Leo III in Rome crowns Charles "Emperor of the West", a title that no sovereign has wielded since the fall of the Western Roman Empire in 476.

Administration

In order to govern his immense empire, Charlemagne and his advisers design a clever administrative system, based on mutual allegiance and assistance. Members of the Frankish elite take on administrative, judicial, and war tasks. They literally assist their monarch "in work and deed", in exchange for which they are remunerated with country estates. Charles divides his empire in counties headed by an official, the Count. Inspectors regularly visit to check each Count's administration by reference to a standard questionnaire, whereupon they report to Charles. The main laws for each region are set down in decrees: the *capitularia*.

Charles owns several residences spread across his empire, the so-called "palaces". Presumably, he also had a palace in Nijmegen, the Valkhof. Charles travels from palace to palace, taking care of local administrative and judicial matters. Several times a year, the leading residents of the entire empire meet in such a palace, during so-called "diets", to decide on important military and administrative issues. The visits to the palaces also constitute a form of taxation in kind: to accommodate

Charles and his extensive royal household during their sojourn, the staff draw on the supplies and resources of the region.

Charles sets great store by education, culture, and science. He orders the foundation of schools where young men are educated for public service, and he receives scholars from many countries in his court. There is no need for him to write – he leaves writing to his officials – but he is an excellent reader. He is also well versed in mathematics and astronomy, and he speaks several languages. Charles introduces a common currency which is accepted all across his empire, and an easily readable and writable typeface, the Carolingian Minuscule.

Charles also establishes diplomatic relations in the Muslim world. In 797, a Jewish envoy travels to the Caliph in Baghdad, Harun al-Rashid. Five years later, he returns with a range of gifts for Charles, among which is an elephant by the name of Abul-Abbas.

Stories

Charles spends the last years of his life in his palace in Aachen. Here, he dies in 814. He is laid to rest in the palace chapel, which constitutes the foundation of the current Aachen Cathedral. In 1165, Charles is canonised. He goes down in history as one of the greatest rulers ever. Even during his lifetime, he is the subject of many stories going round, which are embellished after his death.

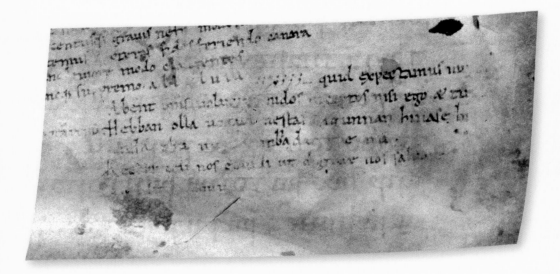

Hebban olla vogala

The Dutch language under development

'Hebban olla vogala nestas hagunnan hinase hic anda thu' is one of the best-known sentences in the history of Dutch language and literature. The next line reads "Wat unbidan we nu?". Its meaning: "All the birds are already nesting, except for me and you. What are we waiting for?" These are two lines from a medieval love song. A song of longing, some thousand years old.

Mystery

'Hebban olla vogala nestas hagunnan hinase hic anda thu. Wat unbidan we nu?' These thirteen words are famous yet shrouded in mystery. We know that they were written down around 1075 but we do not know for certain who the author

is and which dialect he is using.

Most probably, the author is a monk from Flanders. At that time, he has already been living and working for quite a while in a monastery in Kent, in southern England.

A large proportion of his working day is spent copying Latin and Old English texts. This is done in the scriptorium: a room with desks and all the materials required to write, such as parchment, ink, and quills. Every now and then, the quill that the monk is using needs sharpening. Before he continues his task, he tries out his newly sharpened pen on a separate piece of paper. When trying out your pen, you often write something that just happens to come to mind. For the monk, it is a rhyme that he perhaps remembers from his childhood in Flanders: *"Hebban olla vogala…"*

Old Dutch

At that time, the Dutch language has been developing for centuries. The earliest words and fragments from the Low Countries date back to the sixth century. In those days, Dutch is primarily a spoken language rather than a written language. Words written in Dutch rarely emerge. In many cases, they involve individual words in an otherwise Latin text. Or it is an Old Dutch translation of a Bible quote, such as *"Thie wingardon bluoyent anda thie bluom macot suoten stank"* ("The vineyards are blossoming, and the flower is spreading a sweet scent").

Recognising Dutch in the old sentence "Hebban olla vogala" is far from easy. Perhaps it is a mix of Old Dutch, North Sea Germanic, and Kentish. In those days, Germanic languages such as German, Frisian, English, and Dutch resemble one another more closely than they do now. From the very beginning, the Dutch language and literature develop in continuous contact with the neighbouring peoples.

Influence

Over the past centuries, Dutch has primarily been influenced by French and Latin, and to a lesser extent, by German. Currently, new words and phrases frequently derive from English and the languages spoken by immigrants, such as Surinamese, Moroccan-Arabic, Turkish, and Berber.

The Hanseatic League

Collaboration pays off

In the late Middle Ages, the cities of Zwolle, Kampen, Zutphen, and Deventer develop into leading trade hubs. They are members of the Hanseatic League: initially, a merchant confederation and from 1356, also a trade network of cities. The League fosters the expansion and protection of the cities' own trade activities. In the sixteenth century, the Hanseatic League is dissolved.

Trade union

Between the twelfth and sixteenth centuries, a number of Dutch cities, most of them situated in the eastern part of the country, develop into important and prospering trade centres. They owe their position to their membership of the Hanseatic League.

Originally, the Hansa is an alliance between merchants from different cities trading in the same products. Collaboration enables them to cut their costs, travel collectively and therefore more safely, procure or sell on a wider scale, and collectively oppose decisions made by powerful rulers.

In 1356 a meeting is held in Lübeck, a town in what is now modern-day Germany. At this meeting it is decided that the Hanseatic League must become an association of cities, promoting urban interests, rather than a mere confederation of merchants. The Hanseatic League evolves into a powerful network of trading centres in the area bordering on the North Sea and the Baltic Sea. Within this network, the League attempts to solve trade issues wherever it can. The Hanseatic network also trades with partners outside its territory, for example, with London and with Spanish cities.

Expansion and boom
The trade in products such as salt, grains, fish, wood, wine, beer, animal skins, and cloth flourishes. The goods are largely transported by sea and by rivers, using cog ships of between fifteen to thirty metres in length. The cities blossom, reinforce their city walls, expand their ports, and become dotted with merchant homes, warehouses, and offices. The riches of the Hanseatic League are still clearly manifest in the aforementioned cities along the River IJssel, but also in smaller Hanseatic cities such as Stavoren, Hasselt, Tiel, and Doesburg.

Confidence
The Hanseatic cities gain confidence. In order to promote trade over land, in 1448 the Kampen city administration commissions the construction of a bridge across the River IJssel, without requesting permission from the bishop, the local sovereign. The new bridge is built within five months. The toll that each passing ship is required to pay flows into the city coffers.

Deventer and other Hanseatic towns around the Rivers IJssel and Rhine protest against this measure. They want free passage along the River IJssel and even complain to the bishop's superior: Emperor Frederick III of the German Empire. He sends the city a letter ordering the demolition of the bridge. However, Kampen refuses to oblige. The Emperor and the bishop do not pursue the matter any further and the bridge stays put.

Mother of all trade
Trade to the Baltic Sea is also vitally important for non-Hanseatic cities such as Amsterdam. This trade forms the basis for the economic boom. Amsterdam is mainly trading in bulk goods such as grain and wood but has to compete with the IJssel cities. During the sixteenth century the power of the Hanseatic League declines. Holland is gaining economic strength at the expense of the IJssel cities that are hampered by a silting river. Only after the fall of Antwerp, in 1585, does Amsterdam become a truly important trade centre. Dutch trade becomes increasingly focused on the world seas. However, the trade to the Baltic Sea remains of such paramount importance to the Dutch economy and its food supply that it is referred to as the "mother of all trade".

1450? – 1516

Hieronymus Bosch

Painter in a medieval town

Towards the end of the Middle Ages, the city of 's-Hertogenbosch houses an artist with a remarkably creative fantasy. His paintings and drawings warn against the consequences of human sin and folly, as is common in those days. At the same time, Hieronymus Bosch boasts a figurative language that is unique and unforgettable.

The medieval city

Hieronymus Bosch lives and works on the Markt square in the Dutch city of 's-Hertogenbosch, also referred to as Den Bosch. In the fifteenth century, the city's economy flourishes, mainly as a result of the production of and trade in metal objects and textiles, such as linens and worsted cloths, and metal objects such as knives and pins. When the Duke of Brabant enfranchises 's-Hertogenbosch in 1185, a wall is built around the Markt square. Here, tradesmen sell all sorts of products.

Trade and industry blossom and increasingly more craftsmen, merchants, and artists settle in 's-Hertogenbosch. Thus, the city expands rapidly. In the fourteenth century, a new city wall is built, approximately surrounding the area of the current city centre.

The Christian faith is extremely important in medieval daily life. The clergy plays a key part in housing the homeless, writing and copying books, teaching children, and taking care of the sick. From the end of the thirteenth century onwards, hospital nurses tend to sick paupers, travellers, and pilgrims in the Groot Gasthuis.

On account of its many churches, monasteries and convents, which attract large numbers of pilgrims, Den Bosch is also dubbed "Little Rome". The most famous of these churches is St. John's Cathedral. Here, Hieronymus Bosch is a member of *De Illustre Lieve Vrouwe Broederschap* (the Illustrious Brotherhood of Our Blessed Lady), a religious association that commissions him to paint several paintings. In addition, he is commissioned by influential noblemen and sovereigns.

The Garden of Earthly Delights

Although his family name is Van Aken, Hieronymus Bosch signs several of his paintings as "Jheronimus Bosch". With his art, he aims to admonish people to live as good, faithful Christians, otherwise things will turn out badly after their death.

His most famous painting is *The Garden of Earthly Delights*. This large triptych tells the story of mankind from Creation onwards. The left panel shows the first humans, Adam and Eve. The middle panel features countless naked women and men in a paradise setting.

On the right, devils in Hell are torturing the sinful souls of the deceased, topped by one of Bosch's iconic city fires. As a child, he probably witnessed a huge city fire in 1463, during which more than four hundred wooden houses in Den Bosch went up in flames.

His other works also feature devilish monsters and bizarre creatures, such as flying fish and other imaginary animals, pictured in great detail against strange backdrops. This gains Bosch the nickname "the devil maker". In the early days of the Revolt, the *Garden of Earthly Delights* hangs in William of Orange's palace in Brussels. Here, it is confiscated by Philip II and taken to Madrid, where it is still on display.

Work

Some 25 paintings are credited to Hieronymus Bosch. These are on display in major museums around the globe, for example, in Washington, Vienna, Madrid, Lisbon, and Venice. Only two original pieces are on display in the Netherlands, *The Wayfarer* and *St. Christopher*, in Museum Boijmans Van Beuningen in Rotterdam. Consequently, it was a unique occasion when, in 2016, the 500th anniversary of his death, nearly all his works of art were on view in the city in which he has lived and worked. This exhibition in the Noordbrabants Museum in 's-Hertogenbosch was visited by nearly half a million people.

Hieronymus Bosch has inspired many subsequent painters. His influence is manifest in, e.g., the several famous paintings made by Pieter Brueghel in the sixteenth century, such as *Mad Meg*, but also in the surrealist paintings by Salvador Dalí in the twentieth century.

1457-1482

Mary of Burgundy

Sovereign between Burgundy and Habsburg

Mary of Burgundy is only 25 years old when she dies. Yet her short reign as Duchess marks a significant turning point in the history of the Low Countries. Mary is pressured into restoring rights to her subjects and the Netherlands will continue to be part of the Habsburg empire for a long period of time.

Only a girl

Mary is born in Brussels in 1457, the only child of Isabella of Bourbon and Charles of Charolais. She is the granddaughter of the Duke of Burgundy, Philip the Good. She is baptised with all sorts of pomp and circumstance, but her grandfather chooses not to attend the ceremony because she is only a girl. However, as his only grandchild, Mary would later become his sole heir.

Through a smart marriage, power politics, and wars, the House of Burgundy manages to expand their duchy substantially, annexing, e.g., the richest parts of the Low Countries, such as Flanders and Brabant. Philips the Good pressures his cousin, Countess Jacqueline of Hainaut, to cede her counties Zeeland and Holland to him when she dies. Philip also sets up the Estates General: a political body in which all the constituent territories of the Burgundian Netherlands are represented.

Following his death in 1467, Philip is succeeded by his son Charles. Charles is continually on the warpath, seeking to expand his territories even further. This earns him his nickname, "the Bold". Mary is often accompanied by her stepmother, Margaret of York, sister to the King of England. The two of them undertake many diplomatic travels on behalf of the Duke. His costly wars continue to undermine Charles' popularity. Furthermore, he takes on increasingly more authority, which does not go down well with the Estates General.

Duchess

In January 1477, Charles dies on the battlefield and Mary, the brand-new Duchess of Burgundy, becomes Europe's richest heiress. The French King Louis XI immediately seizes the opportunity to re-annex the Burgundian territories, which he claims belong to the French crown. He justifies his action by stating that a woman cannot be a vassal to the King of France. He attempts to force Mary to marry his son.

Mary is forced to take two steps to avoid French rule. In order to secure the support of the Burgundy territories, she signs the Great Privilege. Under this agreement, she returns the rights of the various regions that her father has annexed. In exchange for these privileges, the Estates General are to pledge their allegiance and agree to new war taxes. In addition, she follows her father's wish and marries Maximilian of Austria, of the Habsburg dynasty. In Maximilian, she has a powerful monarch to protect her territories.

Her marriage marks the end of Mary's political career. As is customary at the time, from now on she must leave all political decisions to her husband. Bearing children for the dynastic succession now constitutes her main task, and within a short period of time she has three children. As many of her wealthy contemporaries, Mary commissions a "book of hours". She uses this beautifully adorned prayer book for her daily devotion to God. In 1482, Mary dies, a few weeks after a horseriding accident. She is laid to rest in a beautiful tomb, which can still be visited in Bruges.

Legacy

Following Mary's marriage, large sections of the Low Countries become part of the Habsburg Empire, which would later extend into Asia and the Americas. In the sixteenth century, her grandson Charles V gains dominion of this world empire. The Great Privilege is not forgotten, nor are other agreements with the territories. A century later, they are a source of inspiration in the Revolt against Mary's great-grandson Philip II.

1469?-1536

Erasmus

A critical mind in Europe

Desiderius Erasmus is both a critical philosopher and a conciliator. This influential humanist's best-known work by far is In Praise of Folly, a satirical attack on the Roman Catholic Church. Yet when the Protestants secede, Erasmus continues to advocate religious reform from within the church.

Desiderius Erasmus is born around 1469, son to an unmarried priest and his housekeeper. His youth is spent in several boarding schools. Subsequently, he ends up in Paris, where he studies theology. Erasmus has an excellent command of Latin and Greek and knows a great deal about classical antiquity.

Even in his own times, he is regarded as a great scholar.

Humanism
Erasmus is a leading humanist. The humanist philosophy revolves around the human existence. As a human being, you need to

In these surroundings, William becomes well acquainted with international political relations and amasses a comprehensive network. For example, he writes some 13,000 letters to his international contacts. Many of these letters are written in French or in his mother tongue, German.

Noble opposition

From 1555 onwards, William of Orange is appointed to high positions. Philip II, the son of Charles V, delegates him to conduct important international negotiations. As a military commander in chief, member of the Dutch Council of State (the monarch's advisory council), Knight of the Order of the Golden Fleece, and stadtholder of Holland, Zeeland, and Utrecht, he becomes one of the most influential noblemen in the Low Countries. His relationship with Philip II, however, is deteriorating. William of Orange becomes the main spokesman for the noble opposition party. He urges the King to ease up on the persecution of heretics and resists the greater role of professional officials in the national government. These new officials are causing noblemen to lose their traditional positions.

Revolt

Resistance against the Spanish ruler is growing. Diplomatic efforts bear little fruit, and in 1566 the Iconoclastic Fury breaks out. Philip II responds by appointing the Duke of Alva, who severely punishes the rebels. William of Orange flees to Dillenburg castle, where from 1568 onwards, he orchestrates several military invasions to end Alva's rule in the Netherlands. In addition, he continues

his battle in the Low Countries by means of propaganda such as pamphlets, militant songs, and prints. The current Dutch national anthem, the *Wilhelmus*, was originally such a propaganda song. Initially, military success is sustained. Only when the *Geuzen* [Beggars], as the rebels call themselves, conquer Den Briel on 1 April 1572, does the Revolt start to garner wider support.

Against all odds, the rebels stand their ground in Holland and Zeeland, which in part can be attributed to William of Orange's perseverance. With the Pacification of Ghent in 1576, they even manage to make peace with the other provinces. William's ideal appears within reach: the restoration of the seventeen provinces under noble rule and ending the battle between the various groups on the basis of tolerance. However, this unity does not last.

Republic

In 1580, Philip places a bounty on William of Orange's head. William responds by writing his Apology (defending his course of action), and the States General of the rebel provinces produce the Act of Abjuration. The argument in the two documents is the same: resistance is justified because the King is acting as a tyrant. On 10 July 1584, Catholic Balthasar Gerards shoots and kills William of Orange. William's efforts appear to have been in vain. However, a few years after his death, the rebel provinces develop into an independent, self-confident republic. That is the reason why in retrospect, William of Orange is considered the founder of this new state, the "Father of the Fatherland".

1547–1619

Johan van Oldenbarnevelt

Chasms within the Republic

After the Northern Netherlands have separated from Philip II,
they restructure as a republic. Grand Pensionary Johan van Oldenbarnevelt
turns this form of government into a success, an achievement that
few countries have managed at that time.

Rise of the Republic

Once the Northern Netherlands cease to acknowledge King Philip II as their sovereign, their attempts to find a new sovereign fail. In 1588, the States General, representing the rebellious territories, decide to adopt sovereignty themselves and form the government of the Republic of the Seven United Netherlands. Several other republics exist, such as Venice and Genoa, but in an era during which monarchs increasingly tend to seek absolute power, this remains an unusual constitution.

Chief official of Holland

Johan van Oldenbarnevelt, born in the Dutch city of Amersfoort, rapidly gets ahead in the district of Holland. He is the confidante of stadtholder William of Orange. In 1586, he is appointed Grand Pensionary (also referred to as Land's Advocate) of the States of Holland, which makes him their chief official. He turns the Republic into a well-functioning entity.

Holland is wealthy and, as the district that brings in the most money, it also holds the largest vote in the Republic. Van Oldenbarnevelt ensures that he becomes the key figure in the States General. His leadership enables the States General effectively to levy taxes and carry out a successful offensive against Spain. He pursues political compromises and if he fails, he tackles his opponents with bribery, threats, and military power. Furthermore, he initiates the establishment of a trade organisation, the Dutch East India Company. Van Oldenbarnevelt operates as a type of Prime Minister, Finance Minister, and Foreign Affairs Minister all at the same time. He is well respected at home and abroad and is regarded as the driving force of the Republic.

Conflict and beheading

Eventually, Van Oldenbarnevelt is faced with a rival: stadtholder Prince Maurice, the son of William of Orange. A stadtholder (literal meaning: deputy) is appointed by the monarch to govern on his behalf, but as a republic does not have a monarch, this original task is now defunct. Formally, the stadtholder is no more than a servant to the States General. However, as a leading aristocrat and supreme commander of the armed forces, Maurice towers far above all the other administrators.

For a long time, the Republic flourishes under their joint rule. Van Oldenbarnevelt focuses on politics, whilst Maurice limits himself to his military role tasks – a perfect collaboration, or so it seems. However, after 1600, they regularly clash. Maurice wants to continue to wage war against Spain, whereas Van Oldenbarnevelt signs a truce, the Twelve Years' Truce (1609-1621).

In addition, the Grand Pensionary wants to prevent religious quarrels within the Protestant church. He appears willing to call in army troops to enforce his intentions. Thus, he encroaches upon the stadtholder's domain. Maurice feels threatened and removes Van Oldenbarnevelt's authority. Eventually, he has him arrested. To his own astonishment, the Grand Pensionary is sentenced to death on a charge of high treason. On 13 May 1619, Van Oldenbarnevelt is beheaded on a scaffold in front of the Knights' Hall in The Hague. This drama is exacerbated by the fact that his conviction is initiated by the son of his hero, William of Orange.

Johan van Oldenbarnevelt has been instrumental in the expansion of the Republic to one of the main powers within Europe. However, the power struggle between the Grand Pensionaries and the stadtholders of the House of Orange still continues for quite some time.

Dutch East India Company and Dutch West India Company

Sailing and fighting for trade

Seventeenth-century Europe sees a growing demand for luxury products from overseas: spices, sugar, coffee, tea, and china. Merchants jostle to meet this demand. For small businesses, however, long-distance journeys to Asia, Africa or the Americas are costly and dangerous. New corporations are established to organise this overseas trade.

Dutch East India Company

On 2 April 1595, three trade vessels – the Mauritius, Hollandia, and Amsterdam – and a small yacht – the *Duyfken* – set sail for Asia, departing from the island of Texel.

It is a high-risk venture; only three of the four vessels and but 87 of the 249 crew return in August 1597. The proceeds are slim, but nonetheless this "first expedition" to Asia is an economic success. The Dutch have opened a new trade route, after Spain and Portugal had already discovered this sea route.

In 1602, Johan van Oldenbarnevelt establishes the Dutch East India Company (in Dutch: *Vereenigde Oostindische Compagnie* or VOC) in the purview of the trade with Asia. The British, French, and other European countries have similar corporations at that time, but the VOC becomes the largest by far. The VOC attains the Dutch monopoly on all the trade in the Asian waters east of the Cape of Good Hope. The Republic has authorised the VOC to sign treaties, wage war, and govern conquered areas on its behalf. From all over Europe, young men travel to the Republic to enlist with the VOC. A large proportion of them never see Europe again. They die of illnesses breaking out on board during the long voyages.

The VOC develops into a dreaded power and war machine. It builds fortresses in places such as the current South Africa, India, Sri Lanka, and Makassar. These outposts are used to conduct trade activities and to defend its trade areas. In certain countries, the VOC secures a special position. When Japan is closed off to all foreigners, the VOC is the only entity, in 1641, to get permission to trade, from the island of Deshima near Nagasaki.

Jan Pieterszoon Coen
In 1619, Jan Pieterszoon Coen, the fourth Governor-General of the VOC, conquers the city of Jayakarta, where he establishes Batavia. He has parts of Java occupied. Ambon and Ternate on the Molucca Islands are forced into subjection. The local population is forced to cultivate spices. When in 1621 the inhabitants of the Banda Islands revolt against the VOC, Coen has nearly the entire population massacred, enslaving any survivors. From the 15,000 Banda people, not even a thousand remain on one of the islands.

Dutch West India Company
In 1621, the Dutch West India Company (in Dutch: *West-Indische Compagnie* or WIC) is established. The States General awards the Company the exclusive rights to colonisation, trade, and privateering in the areas around the Atlantic Ocean. The WIC rules colonies such as New Netherlands in North America, Brazil, and slave colonies in the Caribbean. Its attempts to build an empire similar to that of the VOC fail. Because distances across the Atlantic Ocean are relatively short, competitors manage to break through the WIC's monopoly position. Eventually, the WIC only retains the right to the slave trade and the rule over several smaller colonies, such as the trade hubs in the Caribbean and Africa.

For decades, the two Companies stock Dutch warehouses with colonial products, and fill residential homes with rare objects from an unknown world. By the end of the eighteenth century, the WIC and the VOC are disbanded as a result of such factors as declining profits, competition, corruption, and wars.

World Heritage
Currently, the archives of the two Companies feature on the World Heritage List. The letters to and from administrators, reports on negotiations with kings and rulers in Asia, the Americas, and Africa, and the extensive staff records constitute an important source for research into and discussion about colonial and trade histories.

1612

The Beemster

Dry feet in the polder

At the beginning of the seventeenth century, the Beemster is still a large lake in the province of North Holland. In 1607, the authorities decide to impolder the lake so that farmers may grow crops there. The Beemster has since been a symbol for the way in which the Dutch are taking control over the topography of their country.

World Heritage

In 1607, the Provincial Council of Holland and West Friesland grants permission to impolder Lake Beemster. It has all the signs of becoming a lucrative project; moreover, it can contribute to providing food for the fast-growing city of Amsterdam. The first step involves surrounding the lake with a high and robust dyke, 38 kilometres in length. Around this dyke, a ring canal is dug. Subsequently, the lake is pumped dry, which requires no fewer than 43 windmills. Engineer Jan Adriaenszoon Leeghwater is co-responsible for the construction and the placement of the windmills. The process requires several windmills in a row, each of which pump the water a little higher, until it reaches the ring canal.

In 1612, the lake is dry, and the polder can be planned. Roads are constructed, ditches are dug, and farmhouses are built. Everything is designed in a well-structured, austere geometric pattern. It is to this way of parcellation and land allocation that the Beemster Polder owes its fame.

The Netherlands is shaped by human intervention in nature. This intervention starts as early as the sixth century BC, with the construction of terps and mounds that enable living in safety. Land reclamation follows in the Middle Ages, increasingly more dykes are constructed and regional water boards are set up. From the sixteenth century onwards, water management is pursued on an even larger scale and in a more systematic manner, by impoldering lakes and peat pools. The Beemster is currently on the UNESCO World Heritage List. This polder is a textbook example of how Dutch people have "created" large parts of their country with their own hands.

Water management
In the centuries that follow, water management in the Beemster polder continues to develop. For a long time, windmills ensure that residents keep their feet dry, and that the polder level remains low enough for land cultivation. In the late nineteenth century, the windmills are replaced by steam-driven pumping stations. Subsequently, diesel pumping stations and electrically driven pumps take over. The Beemster polder is currently divided into more than fifty sections, each featuring its own water level. Crop farmers need a low water level underneath their fields, whereas villagers prefer a high level in order to prevent the piles underneath their homes from rotting. The ideal water level for cattle farmers is somewhere in between, whilst nature managers have yet other requirements.

In the past, water was only pumped away to prevent waterlogging. Nowadays, during periods of drought, fresh water from Lake IJsselmeer – the former Zuiderzee – is let into the Beemster. After the Zuiderzee was closed off from the sea, this body of water turned into a freshwater lake, whose water is used for agricultural purposes. Once upon a time, wind power and windmills turned water into land in the Beemster polder; nowadays, modern water management is carried out there using electricity and computers.

More new land
After the seventeenth century, impoldering continues in the Netherlands. In 1852, Lake Haarlemmermeer is pumped dry. This is the first lake to be drained entirely by using steam power. One of the three pumping stations used in the process is the Cruquius, featuring the world's largest steam engine. Reclamation of the North East Polder and the Flevo Polder in the former Zuiderzee produces the province of Flevoland. The Netherlands has since built an international reputation in terms of dredging and water management. At several locations across the globe, Dutch businesses are creating new land, such as the artificial Palm Islands near Dubai.

1583 - 1645

Hugo Grotius

Pioneer of modern international law

The King of France calls him "the miracle of Holland".
Hugo Grotius is a brilliant jurist, who lays the foundation for
international law. In 1619, he is imprisoned at Loevestein Castle
by his political enemy, Prince Maurice. With assistance from his wife,
Grotius manages to escape in a book chest.

A child prodigy

Hugo Grotius is born in 1583 into an influential family residing in Delft. Only eleven years old, he enrols in the newly founded university in Leiden to read law. Young Grotius turns out to be an intellectual all-rounder, writing Latin verses with the same ease as arranging the publication of writings from classical antiquity. At the age of fifteen, Hugo Grotius accompanies Grand Pensionary Johan van Oldenbarnevelt on a diplomatic mission to the French court, in order to garner support for the Dutch revolt against Spain. The French King speaks very highly of him.

Imprisonment and escape

During the Twelve Year Truce (1609-1621), a political and religious conflict in the newly established Dutch Republic escalates. Johan van Oldenbarnevelt takes a stand against stadtholder Prince Maurice. As Van Oldenbarnevelt's advisor, Grotius becomes one of the leading figures in this conflict. In 1618, Maurice has his opponents imprisoned. By Maurice's order, Van Oldenbarnevelt is sentenced to death, whilst Grotius is imprisoned for life in Loevestein Castle, near the town of Gorinchem, where his family joins him.

In 1621, his wife Maria van Reigersberch devises a plan to help Grotius escape. He is regularly provided with books from Gorinchem, which are delivered and collected in a chest. On 22 March, Maria and her maidservant Elsje van Houweningen place the delivered books in Grotius's bed, making it seem as though he is lying there. Grotius climbs into the chest, which is carried out the castle and taken to Gorinchem. Subsequently, he flees to Antwerp, dressed as a bricklayer. He spends the rest of his life in exile abroad and dies in 1645 in Rostock.

International law

His escape marks the end of Grotius's time in Holland, but not the end of his intellectual activities and reputation as a scholar. In addition to literary works, he writes a large number of treatises on theological, historical, and especially legal topics, among which is *De iure belli ac pacis* ("On the Law of War and Peace"), which explains the principles of international law. With his work, Hugo Grotius lays the foundation for international law as we know it. For example, he describes the circumstances under which a state is justified in declaring war on another state, and what means are permitted in battle. Furthermore, in his opinion, any violence exerted must always be proportional to its purpose.

Story

Throughout the ages, Grotius's escape in a book chest continues to fire imaginations. As a victim of the stadtholder, he joins the ranks of Van Oldenbarnevelt and the brothers Johan and Cornelis de Witt in personifying opposition to the Oranges. During the Patriot period, several objects turn up that are claimed to have been his, among which are several book chests. One such chest is on display in the Rijksmuseum in Amsterdam; others are held by Museum Het Prinsenhof in Delft and Loevestein Castle.

1637

The *States Bible*

The power of the Word

Many Christians regard the Bible as the most important book, because it is "the Word of God". The States Bible, the Dutch Authorised Translation of the Bible, dating from 1637 has been authoritative for centuries. Large groups of faithful have become familiar with its language. This Bible has embedded such expressions as "forbidden fruit" and "thorn in one's flesh" into the Dutch language.

Belief on the basis of the Bible

Most medieval Christians regard the rituals (recurrent, solemn acts) of the church as far more important than reading the Bible. This is not surprising, considering that in those days, few people know how to read and write.

With the rise of the middle classes, literacy booms. A fertile soil develops for the idea of reformists such as Martin Luther (1483-1546) that belief on the basis of the Bible holds more importance than the rituals. More and

44

more of the faithful grow convinced that it is imperative to be able to read the Bible individually, and that the main task of the clergy is to explain the Bible.

As early as the Middle Ages, sections of the Bible are translated into Dutch. One such example is Jacob van Maerlant's Rhyming Bible, dating from 1271. Around 1535, Martin Luther translates the Bible into German; for his translation, he uses Erasmus's edition of the Greek New Testament. The sixteenth century sees several Dutch translations of Luther's German translation.

New translation

The newly established Republic perceives a growing need for a national language and a national Bible to settle its religious differences. The Protestant Church develops a demand for a new Bible translation, patterned on the English Authorized Version: the King James Bible that was published in 1611. In 1618, an important church assembly, the Synod of Dordrecht, decides to commission a new translation of the Bible. The translation is to be funded by the States General; hence, it is commonly referred to as the States Translation. The Synod orders the translators to carefully adhere to the original Hebrew and Greek texts, and to formulate the text in universally comprehensible, clear wording.

As a result of a range of religious and political discussions, the States General does not endorse this proposal until 1626, whereupon the translators commence their work. Nine years later, the translation is completed, and in 1637 the States Translation or States Bible is ready to print. Between 1637 and 1657, as many as half a million copies are printed, to serve a Dutch population of two million.

Influence on the Dutch language

The States Translation is used and read in all seven provinces of the Republic. Throughout the ages, large groups of Protestant believers have become familiar with the language used in the States Bible. Expressions derived from the States Translation, such as "in the sweat of thy face", "forbidden fruit", and "thorn in the flesh" are firmly embedded in the Dutch languages. For a long time, the States Translation has been presumed to have had a major impact on the development of Standard Dutch, but according to recent academic research, this is hardly the case.

Until approximately 1950, the States Bible remains the most widely read Bible translation in the Protestant churches. To this day, some church communities continue to use this translation. In addition, a "Revised States Translation" has been introduced.

1606?-1669

Rembrandt

A country full of painters

According to the calculations, in the seventeenth century, more than five million paintings were made in the Republic: a country full of painters. Paintings adorn the walls of not only the rich, but also those of commoners. The most famous painter of all is Rembrandt, and his best-known painting is *The Night Watch*, dating from 1642.

All walks of life

Rembrandt van Rijn is an ambitious painter, who, at a young age, leaves his birthplace Leiden in the hopes of making a career for himself in the wealthier and bigger city of Amsterdam. His efforts are successful. With his expensive portraits and paintings of Biblical and mythological characters and scenes, he serves the elite of well-to-do-citizens and art connoisseurs. In addition, Rembrandt draws and paints many local inhabitants of Amsterdam, among whom are immigrants. The vicinity of his

Jodenbreestraat studio is home to dozens of sailors and soldiers of African descent. This is reflected in many of his paintings, e.g., *Two African Men* (1661).

The Night Watch

Rembrandt's painting *The Night Watch* is world famous. It is a fine example of his painting style. He creates depth by his iconic use of light and dark, which is also referred to as chiaroscuro or clair-obscure. The painting dates from 1642 and has since been widely discussed and acclaimed. It is indeed an intriguing painting: something is about to happen, but what? On the other hand, it is quite an ordinary painting: a group of Amsterdam residents gathered around their Captain Frans Banninck Cocq, posing for a group portrait intended for the new banquet hall of the newly renovated *Kloveniersdoelen*, the musketeers' meeting hall in Amsterdam. The group portrait tradition in Amsterdam dates back to the first half of the sixteenth century. Captain Banninck Cocq's fellow officers follow suit and also commission group portraits from renowned painters. Thus, Rembrandt's painting initially hangs amidst several new group portraits in the hall in which the militia regularly gather to collectively eat, drink, and smoke.

Over the past centuries, *The Night Watch* has been through quite a lot: from requisite relocations to vandalism. In 2018, the Rijksmuseum announces a large-scale restoration: Operation Night Watch. The operation involves a thorough inspection in order to explore, among other things, how the painting can best be preserved for future generations.

The art market

Rembrandt is not the only symbol of the remarkable cultural flourishing of the seventeenth century; he is joined by Johannes Vermeer, Frans Hals, Jan Steen, and all those other hundreds of local painters. Around 1650, some 175 painters are active in Amsterdam alone. A majority of them produce cheap little paintings for an anonymous market, usually landscapes and representations of everyday scenes. Although it has not earned them eternal fame, their work is a mark of the scope of the Dutch art of painting. Calculations have revealed that more than five million paintings must have been made in the seventeenth century. In those days, the population figure of the Republic fluctuates around two million.

Painting is not the only art to flourish in this period of time; literature blossoms too. Writers such as Joost van den Vondel and Pieter Corneliszoon Hooft have contributed to this period's place in history as the golden age of art.

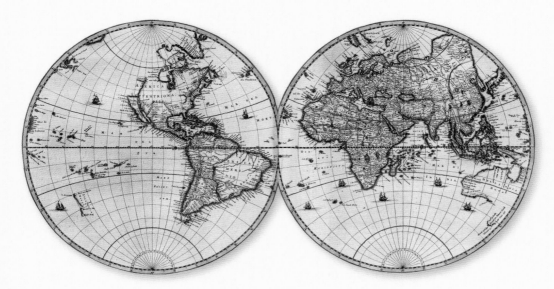

1662

Blaeu's *Atlas Maior*

Mapping the world

In the sixteenth century, European seafarers and explorers start to map out many unknown areas. The prosperous Republic harbours a great demand for luxury and detailed world maps, such as the ones produced by Willem Blaeu and his son. The famous *Atlas Maior* from 1662 is their pièce de resistance.

Cartographers

The atlases and maps printed in the seventeenth century in the Blaeu family business in Amsterdam are world famous. Kings, czars, and other rulers of the world, they all want one of Blaeu's beautifully designed atlases or fine globes. These symbolise riches

and knowledge, a favoured combination.

Willem Janszoon Blaeu (1571-1638), son of a herring merchant, learns the art of navigation in Denmark as a student of the renowned Danish astronomer Tycho Brahe.

He is trained as an instrument and globe maker. Upon his return to Amsterdam, he sets up his own printshop and publishing house, manufacturing globes and, at a later date, maps. From his very first maps, printed in 1605, Blaeu's quality and innovative approach attract attention. Rather than setting out to conduct his own measurements, Blaeu designs his maps on the basis of existing map material, supplemented with knowledge derived from ships' logs, travel journals, and interviews with sailors. His maps and atlases earn Blaeu international fame.

After his death, his son Joan (1599?-1673) takes over the company. Under his leadership, the family business begins to thrive even more. Eighty employees keep fifteen printing presses running. A considerable number of women and children earn money by colouring in the maps.

Travel maps

Blaeu's maps follow a long tradition. The oldest known maps, made in olden-day China and the Middle East, serve a cadastral purpose: they record land ownership. From Greek and Roman times onwards, maps start to show the world. The first maritime maps date from the thirteenth century. The invention of the compass ensures that ships no longer need to keep sight of the coast in order to keep their bearings.

The Spaniards and Portuguese are the first Europeans to cross and map out the oceans. Good maps make all the difference during wars, or when conquering new areas.

The route to Asia by way of South Africa is long and exhausting. Consequently, finding a faster route will pay off. The young Republic sends Willem Barentsz on an expedition to find a northern passage along the polar circle. In 1596, his attempt founders in the ice near Nova Zembla, but it does yield a wealth of new information for the cartographer to use.

Atlas Maior

Joan Blaeu produces a host of new maps and atlases, among which is the renowned *Atlas Maior* which from 1662 onwards is marketed in several editions and languages. Featuring nearly six hundred maps and several thousands of pages of descriptions, this multi-volume atlas maps out the world as it is known at the time. The *Atlas* shows how voyages of discovery and trade contacts have expanded knowledge of the world. In Blaeu's day and age, the Republic has amassed the most expertise in this field, although its know-how is quickly adopted by cartographers in other countries.

The *Atlas* is the most expensive multi-volume book of the seventeenth century. The uncoloured version costs 350 guilders, more than a craftsman's annual income. The coloured version is even more expensive: 450 guilders. The actual maps are beautifully executed, yet seldom original. Many of them have been published before, some are outdated, and most are not quite accurate. Nonetheless, the *Atlas* is held in great esteem. With his *Atlas Maior*, Blaeu brings the world to everyone's fingertips, in the finest design conceivable.

1607-1676

Michiel de Ruyter
The Republic in choppy seas

Within the Republic, sea captains are considered major heroes.
This also goes for Michiel de Ruyter. In 1667, he is commissioned
to lead a smart politico-military action: the naval raid on Chatham
via the River Thames, intended to destroy British shipyards and ships.
The plan succeeds, and across the globe De Ruyter is acclaimed
as a naval hero.

To sea!

Michiel Adriaenszoon de Ruyter is born in 1607 in Vlissingen, the son of a brewery drayman. From early on it is clear that his future lies at sea. After briefly working as a rope maker, at the age of eleven he signs up as a boatswain's apprentice on his first ship. It is the beginning of a life at sea. He sails the seven seas in various capacities and positions, such as privateer and captain of a merchant vessel. In 1652, he believes his earnings are sufficient to warrant a tranquil life on shore. However, this plan is thwarted by the Anglo-Dutch Wars.

Anglo-Dutch Wars

For a substantial part of the seventeenth century, the Republic is at war. In 1648, the Peace of Münster ends the Eighty Years' War against Spain. Trade conflicts soon result in two naval wars with England. Following the outbreak of the First Anglo-Dutch War (1652-1654), the Admiralty of Zeeland requests De Ruyter to enlist in the navy. He accepts the position, for one voyage only. However, this turns out to be the start of a new career, culminating in the highest position in the navy: that of Lieutenant-Admiral.

In 1667, Grand Pensionary Johan de Witt devises a plan to win the Second Anglo-Dutch War (1665-1667). He has his brother, Cornelis de Witt, join De Ruyter in leading the fleet into the lion's den and defeat the enemy on their own turf. The plan is successful, and a large section of the English fleet is destroyed near Chatham. The English flagship *HMS Royal Charles* is captured and taken back home in triumph. Her transom is now on display in the Rijksmuseum in Amsterdam.

Year of Disaster

The year 1672 has gone down in history as the Year of Disaster. France and England enter into an alliance in order to contain the power of the Republic. After the De Witt brothers are murdered, Prince William III is appointed as the new Stadtholder. Under his rule, De Ruyter defeats the Anglo-French alliance in three successful sea battles. The decisive one is the Battle of Kijkduin on 21 August 1673. Although the Anglo-French fleet is larger and has more ammunition, De Ruyter literally has the wind behind him and sails straight towards the enemy. This aggressive attack wins De Ruyter the battle. The French retreat during the blood bath, which leaves the Dutch fleet virtually without any resistance. Thus, De Ruyter manages to prevent the English from landing ashore.

In 1676, De Ruyter dies near Syracuse in a battle against the French. He is laid to rest in a marble mausoleum in the New Church in Amsterdam.

Image

In the seventeenth century, the administrators of the coastal provinces like to depict the Republic as a peace-loving maritime and trading nation that hates to wage war. In this self-made image, the admirals of the fleet are the great heroes. Their praises are sung in songs, their lives and actions are described in popular history books, and key naval battles are depicted in paintings and prints.

Michiel de Ruyter is still regarded as the best-known admiral in Dutch history. However, his reputation as a naval hero is also under discussion. Although he has freed enslaved European Christians, he has also sailed to the West African coast to protect Dutch trade interests, including the trade in enslaved Africans.

1629 – 1695

Christiaan Huygens
The beginnings of modern science

Christiaan Huygens invents the pendulum clock, he is a leading mathematician, physicist, and astronomer, and he is the first to observe the rings around the planet Saturn. He is one of the first generation of modern scientists in Europe.

Childhood

Christiaan Huygens is born in 1629 as the second son to Suzanna van Baerle and Constantijn Huygens, a poet and secretary to two Princes of Orange. Constantijn Huygens envisages diplomatic careers for his sons and sends them to Leiden and Breda to study law and military science. However, Christiaan takes more of an interest in mathematics, physics, and astronomy. At an early age, he is already engaged in correspondence with authoritative scientists abroad regarding a wide range of issues.

Scientific revolution

Huygens is an admirer of French philosopher René Descartes (1596-1650), the "father of modern philosophy", who has lived in the Netherlands for many years. Descartes does not base his reasoning on existent, sometimes old views and theories. He wants to experiment, observe, and formulate his own principles. This innovative approach to practicing science catches on and sparks a scientific revolution. Huygens follows in Descartes' footsteps. His mathematical approach to scientific problems is to determine the development of the natural sciences. Huygens discusses his findings in regular correspondence with several contemporaries, among whom is Spinoza. He is also a mentor to Antoni van Leeuwenhoek, the inventor of the microscope.

Achievements

Huygens is of major significance to mechanics. He studies falling and oscillatory motions, in 1656 resulting in one of his greatest inventions: the pendulum clock. For several centuries, this is the only accurate timekeeping instrument. Knowing the exact time is of paramount importance for orientation at sea. For that reason, he also works on the production and improvement of naval clocks.

Huygens enjoys wider fame as an astronomer. Together with his older brother Constantijn,

he grinds lenses for microscopes and astronomical field glasses. After building a telescope, Huygens discovers the ring around the planet Saturn and Saturn's moon Titan. Earlier, other scientists had described the peculiar appearance of the planet as "a type of little ears". Christiaan discovers it is actually a ring.

International esteem

Huygens spends a great deal of time in England and France. In 1655, he earns a PhD at the University of Angers, and in 1666, he is appointed principal of the Académie Royale des Sciences in Paris. From 1681 until his death in 1695, his abode alternates between Hofwijck in the Dutch town of Voorburg – the country estate that was designed by his father – and his home on the Plein Square in The Hague.

After Huygens, Dutch science retains its high esteem and position within international networks. The fame of renowned physician Herman Boerhaave (1668-1738) extends to China. Around 1900, many Nobel prizes are awarded to Dutch scientists. One of them is famous physicist Hendrik Lorentz (1853-1928), whose work lays the foundation for Albert Einstein's theory of relativity.

1632 – 1677

Spinoza

In search of truth

In his own time, Spinoza's body of thought encounters a great deal of resistance. Spinoza believes that Nature – everything that exists, i.e., including mankind – is a manifestation of God. To the people of the seventeenth century, this is a shocking message. Spinoza is currently regarded as one of the most influential philosophers of Western thought.

Outcast

Benedictus de Spinoza is born in 1632 in Amsterdam as Baruch d'Espinoza, the son of Jewish parents who had fled from Portugal. He is raised in the Jewish religious tradition. At home, he speaks Portuguese; in addition, he learns Dutch, Spanish, Hebrew, and Latin,

the language in which he will later write. He is interested in philosophy and at young age, he already expresses criticism of traditional Jewish views. In his eyes, the Jewish Bible – the Torah – is a product of human fantasy. Furthermore, he refuses to abide by the strict requirements and regulations of Jewish tradition in terms of outward appearance. At the age of 23, he is expelled by Jewish society. Consequently, not even his family members are allowed to associate with him. Perforce he leaves Amsterdam, moving to Rijnsburg and subsequently to The Hague. He earns a living by grinding optical and microscope lenses. One of his principals is Christiaan Huygens.

Tolerance

Spinoza is not the only one anxious to distance himself from established ideas. He is supported by several followers, who join him in separating from philosophical and religious traditions. In his *Tractatus theologico-politicus*, published in 1670, Spinoza gives an initial impetus to a more liberal interpretation of the Bible. He advocates democracy and points out the major importance of fundamental tolerance and freedom of speech. Spinoza publishes the *Tractatus* anonymously, for although the Republic harbours more room for critical views compared to surrounding nations, caution is still imperative.

Spinoza writes and publishes during the First Stadtholderless Era, a period of mounting tensions between Orangists and Republicans, in which the atmosphere becomes increasingly grim. The era reaches rock bottom in the Year of Disaster, 1672. Grand Pensionary Johan de Witt is lynched, along with his brother Cornelis, by an Orangist mob without any interference from the authorities. This shocks Spinoza so deeply that he wants to mark the spot with a placard reading "ultimi barbarorum" ("worst barbarians").

His landlord / friend stops him, thus probably saving his life.

Masterpiece

Spinoza's principal work, the *Ethica*, is published shortly after his death. It describes how people can lessen their suffering and thus serves a practical purpose. Man must learn to recognise that God is not dissociated from His creation: everything that exists – including humankind – is a manifestation of God. To Spinoza, God and Nature are two names for the same reality. One cannot attribute human qualities to God, as is customary in the Jewish and Christian traditions. Spinoza thus distances himself from the idea that God can punish or be a good father.

Spinoza always pursues objectivity. This is reflected in how he designs his work. The *Ethica* is structured as a geometric system, in which Spinoza uses definitions and propositions. Throughout history, many readers have complained that this makes the book very difficult to read. Even then Spinoza still has the last word, because the final sentence of his *Ethica* reads: "All noble things are as difficult as they are rare".

Freedom of speech

Spinoza dies in 1677 in The Hague, of a lung disease caused by his work as a lens grinder. Although his body of thought is considered dangerous in the seventeenth century, in the centuries that follow his work gains wide international appreciation. His ideas on the freedom of thinking and the freedom of speech have been important for modern democracy.

c. 1637–1863

Slavery

Human trafficking and forced labour

From the seventeenth century onwards, Dutch colonists in Asia and the Americas have traded people to work on plantations, in mines, and in homes. These slaves did not get paid and were forced to work. This frequently led to uprisings and escape attempts. The Netherlands does not abolish slavery until 1863.

Fort Elmina

In the fifteenth century, the Portuguese establish the first European colonies based on slavery: in sugar plantations along the African coast and subsequently, on a large scale in Brazil. Other European countries follow suit. Along the African coast, forts are established in the purview of the trade with African kingdoms. The most important Dutch fort is Elmina, in present-day Ghana. The colonists here trade with the Ashanti Kingdom, whose residents abduct people and take prisoners of war. In Elmina, such people are bartered to the Dutch traders for cloth, metal, jewellery, alcohol, gunpowder, and weapons.

Dutch West India Company

Under the command of Governor General Johan Maurits of Nassau-Siegen, the Governor General of Netherlands Brazil, the Republic evolves into an increasingly powerful participant in human trafficking. In 1654, the West India Company loses the Brazil colony and thus a major portion of its market. However, the WIC continues its human trafficking, primarily to English and Spanish colonies. Curaçao becomes the slave trade hub in the Caribbean. Thus, for a short period of time, the Republic becomes the world's biggest slave trader. In Asia, the Dutch also trade hundreds of thousands of people.

After 1750, the trans-Atlantic slave trade accounts for the largest share in terms of human trafficking activities. The Dutch role in the slave trade is diminishing, but the products manufactured by slaves are gaining in economic significance. Around 1770, no less than 19 per cent of imported goods are produced by enslaved labourers, whilst more than 5 per cent of the Dutch economy involves slavery-related activities. Between the fifteenth and the nineteenth centuries, European slave traders transport a total of some twelve million slaves across the Atlantic Ocean, 600,000 of whom are transported in Dutch ships.

Uprising

Slavery-based societies are characterised by extreme inequality and violence. The slave owners have the law on their side and exercise terror in order for a small minority to remain in control. Major and minor resistance is the order of the day. In the rural areas of Surinam, some 95 per cent of the population are held as slaves. Some manage to flee and hide in the jungle. From their hiding places, they continue to wage war on the colonists. These fugitives and their descendants are called maroons. Several maroon communities, such as the Saamaka, Aluku, and Okanisi, still exist.

In 1795, the resistance fighter Tula leads a major uprising in Curaçao. He and his fellow rebels demand freedom, inspired by the ideals of the French Revolution and the successful slave uprising in Saint-Domingue (now Haiti; at the time, a French colony). That same year, the Dutch colonial authorities suppress Tula's revolt. He and his fellow fighters are tortured and executed.

Abolition

By the end of the eighteenth century, outrage against the slave trade is growing. After the successful uprising in Saint-Domingue, the French decide to abolish slavery. The English prohibit the slave trade in 1808, and in 1814 they pressure King William I to follow suit. The abolition of slavery for the Netherlands East Indies is a long time coming: here, slave labour is finally banned in 1860 and in the Atlantic colonies on 1 July 1863.

In the Netherlands, the abolition of slavery is commemorated and celebrated during the annual Keti Koti – Surinamese for "chains broken" – liberation event on 1 July.

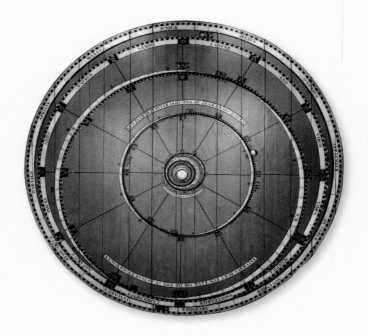

Eise Eisinga

The solar system in a living room

In 1774, the province of Friesland is living in fear that the end of the world is nigh, following a prediction of the earth being thrown out of its orbit. Businessman Eise Eisinga calculates that this is impossible and, as a true Enlightenment thinker, builds a planetarium in his home in Franeker, in order for everyone to see how the solar system works.

Enlightenment thinker

As a child, the highly gifted Eisinga is not allowed to attend Latin School because he is predestined to become a wool comber like his father. Eisinga learns arithmetic from his father's business contacts. He continues to study on his own and focuses on astronomy.

The fact that the University of Franeker (1585-1811) is close by suits him well. For a long time, Eisinga has been presumed to be a humble wool comber, but a recent study has revealed him to be a businessman operating on an international scale. Eisinga employs several men and women, and also trades with the Americas.

As many of his contemporaries, Eisinga is inspired by the Enlightenment. He is convinced that knowledge can improve both mankind and society. Compared to France, Enlightenment reasoning in the Republic is less revolutionary and anti-religious in nature. Adherents of the Dutch Enlightenment tend to believe that God means well by the world. They meet in societies, conducting physics experiments, examining fossils, discussing solutions to societal issues, and studying heavenly bodies.

The planetarium

In 1774, Frisian pastor Eelco Alta publishes a booklet containing a gruesome prediction. Once four planets and the Moon align, their collective gravitational force will pull Earth out of its orbit, to be burned by the Sun. In Friesland, this prediction causes a slight panic. It prompts Eisinga to embark on his planetarium, a job that will take him seven years.

The planetarium that Eisinga constructs in his living room ceiling is a scale model of the solar system. It is completed in 1781. Its central pendulum clock is driven by nine weights. This clock regulates each planet's correct orbital speed via an impressive gear mechanism comprising wooden hoops and discs, featuring 5,934 hand-forged nails as cogs. The speed at which the planets of the planetarium move around the Sun is the same as that of the real planets: Mercury takes 88 days for its orbit, Earth a year, and Saturn more than 29 years.

In addition to an Enlightenment thinker, Eisinga is also a patriot. He opposes the absolutist tendencies of stadtholder William V. When the patriot resistance is broken in 1787, Eisinga is forced to flee. Upon his return to Franeker, he is arrested and exiled from the province for five years. During this time, his family watches over the planetarium for Eisinga to set it in motion again when he returns. In 1818, King William I travels to Friesland to view the planetarium. He is so impressed that he purchases it for the Dutch state. Later on, it is donated to the municipality of Franeker, where the world's oldest working planetarium is still on display.

Instructions

In 1828, Eisinga dies at the age of 84. In his will, he sets out how his planetarium works. To this very day, the planetarium shows the current positions of the planets. The managers still follow Eisinga's instructions, which include the manual re-setting to compensate for a leap day (29 February).

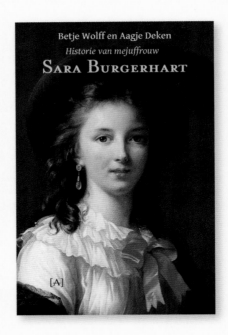

Betje Wolff en Aagje Deken
Historie van mejuffrouw
SARA BURGERHART

[A]

1782

Sara Burgerhart

Rebellious women in the Age of Reason

In 1782, female authors Betje Wolff and Aagje Deken publish a remarkable and original novel. It is the story of nineteen-year-old orphan Sara Burgerhart: a young woman in search of happiness and love. Its contents are revolutionary because the book champions the education of women.

Citizenship

Sara Burgerhart is representative of Dutch Enlightenment, which flourishes in the eighteenth century. The Enlightenment is a broad-based intellectual and cultural movement which regards common sense as a remedy against societal problems. Dutch writers disseminate conventional principles from a Christian perspective. Even though some of their views are rather moderate, they are critical of the existing establishment. For example, they challenge church doctrine and advocate a more active participation of women in the social debate. A main focus is the education of children to become good and virtuous citizens, which is regarded as the basis for a happy and well-balanced society.

Women

Before Wolff and Deken meet in 1776, they are both writing. Elisabeth Wolff-Bekker (1738-1804) is married to a clergyman thirty years her senior and lives in the parsonage of a small village, Middenbeemster. In her study she writes prose and poetry. Her critical poem *De onveranderlyke Santhorstsche geloofsbelydenis* [The Invariable Confession of Faith of Santhorst] (1772), championing liberal religious views, gives rise to much unfavourable comment. Agatha Deken (1741-1804), who grew up in an orphanage in Amsterdam, already has several publications to her credit.

When the women meet, they virtually immediately experience a spiritual connection. When Wolff's husband dies in 1777, they move in together. Their collaboration is highly efficient, and they start publishing as a duo. *Sara Burgerhart* is their best-known work. It is an epistolary novel with autobiographical elements. Its main character, Sara Burgerhart, is an orphan, just like Deken. Just like Wolff, society condemns her because of a failed romantic relationship. In their book, Wolff and Deken write about a theme that holds universal appeal: a young woman's search for happiness in love. Sara goes looking for a suitable marriage partner. After an unsuccessful adventure, she eventually finds the right candidate: Hendrik Edeling.

The message propagated by the authors is revolutionary: marry for love rather than for money. They emphasise that women need to develop their minds and make their own choices. With this archetypal enlightened novel, they intend to encourage "Dutch damsels" to pursue a liberal education. It is essential, however, for such a liberal education to tie in with their role as a woman, which in that day and age differs from the role of a man. Yet this should not prevent women from being able to take part in all types of conversations and present their views on all types of subjects.

Apart from Wolff and Deken, many other women of that time are wielding their pens. In many cases they have to contend with prejudice. This also goes for Isabelle de Charrière, known as Belle van Zuylen in the Netherlands (1740-1805). This daughter of a Dutch noble family writes in French and has women reflect on their underprivileged social position. Her most famous quote is: "I do not have a talent for subservience".

Patriots

Wolff and Deken earn their living by writing and stay true to their patriotic principles. A few years after the publication of their epistolary novel, a patriot rebellion is crushed and they flee from the Netherlands, along with thousands of other patriots. They return after the Batavian Revolution. Both women die in November 1804; they are buried in the same grave in The Hague.

1780–1795

The Patriots

Democratising the Republic

The Republic doesn't amount to anything anymore and the Stadtholder
is to blame. At least, according to the Patriots, who can identify
with the ideals of the Enlightenment. In 1787, they launch
an unsuccessful attempt to assume power. However, in 1795,
France comes to their aid. The Stadtholder is driven away for good.

The decline of the Republic

By the second half of the eighteenth century,
the Golden Age of the Republic seemed
definitely to be over. As a trading nation,
England is outperforming the Republic by far.
The slight growth in the financial sector
does not resolve the vast unemployment.

In terms of international politics, the
Republic hardly counts for anything anymore
either. This becomes painfully clear during
the Fourth Anglo-Dutch War (1780-1784),
which the Republic loses.

Amidst this crisis, a new political group emerges: citizens who, up until then, have had almost no say in national and urban administrations. They blame the decline on the Stadtholder and on corrupt regents. These critical citizens demand involvement and supervision. They call themselves "Patriots" (patriot means fellow country-man). Several regents join their movement.

Revolt

On 26 September 1781, a Patriot in the city of Zwolle by the name of Joan Derk van der Capellen tot den Pol publishes a pamphlet entitled "To the People of the Netherlands", in which he incites the population to revolt. The pamphlet is printed anonymously and secretly distributed across the country in armoured coaches. A political debate ensues in which two parties are formed. On one side, the supporters of Stadtholder William V: the Orangists. On the other, his opponents: the Patriots. Neither camp holds back from using political print. They both inundate the country with magazines, leaflets, and cartoons that analyse and illustrate the condition of the Republic. Slowly but surely, a national feeling emerges. Rather than mere residents of a particular city or region, people start to feel citizens of a country.

Coup d'état

In 1787, the Patriots attempt to assume power and depose the Stadtholder. They organise themselves into "volunteer forces", a type of militias. Stadtholder William V no longer feels safe in the Patriot city of The Hague and retreats to Nijmegen. Within a short time, his wife Wilhelmina of Prussia will play a pivotal role in this *coup d'état*. On 28 June 1787, she travels to The Hague to convince the States of Holland to allow her husband to return. Near Gouda, she is stopped by the Patriots and taken to a farm near the Goejanverwellesluis lock. She claims that the Patriots have treated her in a manner not befitting her status and enlists the help of her brother, King Frederick William II of Prussia, in order to restore Stadtholder power. The Patriot volunteer forces are no match for the well-trained Prussian soldiers. The Stadtholder and his family return, and the Orange dynasty is are once again in power. Following this defeat, many Patriots are imprisoned or attacked by Orangists. For that reason, many of them flee to France.

Batavian Republic

Seven years later, the old Republic comes to an end after all, when the Patriots overthrow the government with the help of the French. The Batavian Republic (1795-1801) is founded, followed by the Batavian Commonwealth (1801-1806). This period sees a range of political reforms, such as the formation of an elected parliament and the introduction of the Netherlands' first Constitution: the Constitution for the Batavian People. In 1806, the Batavian Commonwealth ceases to exist, when Louis Napoleon is crowned King of the Kingdom of Holland.

1769 – 1821

Napoleon Bonaparte

The French period in the Netherlands

Under French rule, freedom is curtailed. France assumes increasingly more power. Emperor Napoleon first appoints his brother Louis Napoleon as King and thereupon annexes the Netherlands into the French Empire. In 1813, Napoleon is defeated by his opponents and the Netherlands regains its independence.

Emperor Napoleon

Napoleon plays a key part in European history. In 1799, he stages a military coup in France. He pursues a vast empire and wages several wars. As a general, he leads his troops on the campaigns against the Emperor of Austria, the Russian Czar, the Sultan of the Ottoman Empire, and the King of England.

In 1804, Napoleon crowns himself Emperor. From 1806 onwards, he rules almost all of Europe, which he governs as an "Enlightened Despot", an absolute sovereign who takes his lead from the ideas of the Enlightenment for as long as he sees fit. He turns the Netherlands into a French vassal state.

territory of the old Republic. Thus, a United Kingdom of the Netherlands is formed: in European terms, a mid-sized country with colonial possessions in several continents.

King-Merchant

During his reign, the energetic William, dubbed "King-Merchant", focuses on restoring the previously thriving economy. To this end, he boosts the economic strengths in the three parts of his Kingdom – the North, the South, and the colonial Dutch East Indies. The South – present-day Belgium – has already seen an industrial revolution and needs to focus on the production of consumer goods. Subsequently, it is up to the tradesmen from the North – now the Netherlands – to transport such products across the globe. The inhabitants of the colonies, finally, are to supply the valuable tropical goods. William I has canals and roads constructed between North and South to facilitate freight transport. These projects are co-funded from his own resources. In 1824, he establishes the Netherlands Trading Company in the purview of the trade with the Dutch East Indies. In this colony, he introduces the cultivation system, requiring the local population to work the fields for a certain period of each year, on behalf of the colonial authorities. Thus, the Dutch East Indies will help to set the economy of the fatherland back on its feet.

The products are sold by the Netherlands Trading Company.

Belgian independence

Despite his economic endeavours, the King is not popular among his southern residents. The Belgian liberals regard him as a ruler who is striving for absolute power and who is not prepared to give the educated elite a greater say. The Belgian Catholics object to the interference of the Protestant King in the training of novice priests. In their opinion, his religious involvement goes too far. The newspapers are increasingly deprived of their journalistic freedom. Furthermore, William demands that Dutch is spoken across much of the country, whereas the Belgian elite mainly speak French.

In 1830, the residents of Brussels revolt. "Death to William I, tyrant of the Netherlands", the Belgian rebels write. William sends an army against them, but to no avail. Belgium regains its independence. Nevertheless, William keeps the army up for another nine years. The high costs that this entails damage the King's popularity in the Netherlands. In 1839, William finally acknowledges Belgian independence. Disillusioned, he abdicates a year later, in favour of his son William II.

1839

The first railway

Acceleration

Is this going to work out, with so much noise and at such a high speed?
In the nineteenth century, the introduction of the train meets with substantial
resistance. However, by 1839, the first railway in the Netherlands is a fact.
The train speeds up life and increases mobility. It connects all the parts of
the country and boosts the manufacturing industry.

The first train journey

On 20 September 1839, the first railway line
in the Netherlands is opened with a festive
celebration. The steam engines named
"Snelheid" [Speed] and "Arend" [Eagle] pull
the first train from Amsterdam to Haarlem
at a speed of 38 kilometres per hour.

Many people wonder whether this novelty
is really necessary and safe, as earlier that
year the steam boiler of a train departing
from Ghent had exploded. Up until 1839,
horse-drawn carriages constitute the fastest
mode of transport; their top speed is some
14 kilometres per hour. Canal vessels provide

68

for a much more comfortable journey, but they travel twice as slowly.

Despite all the initial scepticism, the first train heralds an era of huge change. The Amsterdam-Haarlem line is quickly extended into what is called the "Old Line", running from Amsterdam to Rotterdam. More lines follow, all operated by different railway companies.

Industrialisation

Under the 1860 Railway Act, a substantial expansion of the railway network is funded by the government. The train reaches every location in the Netherlands, which boosts the economy. Raw materials and products need to be transported, and these go easier and faster by train. In the new industrial cities, factories shoot up like mushrooms. Large numbers of people from rural areas move to the cities in search of employment. This urbanisation has a major impact: cities become overcrowded, housing facilities are poor, and the enormous demand for jobs enables factory owners to exploit their employees.

Day tripping by train

By around 1900, the train constitutes the main mode of transport in the Netherlands. Its improved connections and its travel comfort contribute to the unification of the country: it is easier for people from the different regions to come into contact with one another, whilst shorter travel times make the country considerably smaller. Before the advent of railways, travelling was quite tedious, too expensive for most people, and sometimes even dangerous. Ergo, in addition to the infrastructure of the Netherlands, the train also changes residents' perception of their environment.

The train also fosters tourism. Seaside resorts such as Scheveningen and Zandvoort evolve into favourite destinations for spending a day at the beach. New high-speed train connections bring European cities such as Berlin and Paris closer. And conversely, the Netherlands draws a growing number of tourists. Historic towns on the current IJsselmeer Lake are easily accessible by train and thus become tourist attractions, as does Amsterdam, the nation's capital.

The railway network also affects the introduction of a uniform time. For centuries, cities were free to determine their own time. The clocks on church towers in The Hague are ahead of those in Zwolle. That is quite cumbersome for a nationwide timetable, which is why the standard time is introduced in 1909: all over the Netherlands, clocks show the same time.

Environment

At the beginning of the twentieth century, the train meets with fierce competition in terms of passenger and freight transport: the automobile. From the 1930s onwards, many lines are closed, particularly the local ones. However, the train has not disappeared. Despite the advent of the automobile, people have continued to travel by train, for various reasons. Currently, increasingly more people favour the train because of its lower environmental impact, compared to passenger cars or aircraft. Within Europe, old railway connections are being restored as sustainable transport alternatives.

1848

The Constitution

The most important law of the Netherlands

In 1848, William II signs a Constitution that contains considerable curtailment of his royal powers. Less power to the King, more power to the Cabinet and Parliament: the Constitution of 1848 is referred to as the beginnings of the Dutch democracy. However, the history of our Constitution dates back even further.

The Constitution

The Constitution is the most important law of a state. It sets out which individuals and bodies exercise power in the state, and how this is to be effected. For example, the Dutch Constitution sets out the role of the monarch and of the Ministers, the competences of judges, and the tasks of the municipalities and provinces. Furthermore, the Constitution sets out what influence and power Dutch citizens have. No other Acts must conflict with the Constitution.

The Constitution opens with the rights that citizens have in their relation to the state: their basic rights. Rather than those rights that citizens have among and towards one another, basic rights are the rights under which citizens are free to live their lives as they see fit, without state interference in their opinions and life choices. Only if absolutely necessary can the state curtail such liberties as freedom of religion and freedom of speech. Such necessity may arise, for example, if someone presents a danger to others. In such cases, the state may intervene, yet only in accordance with the law.

1798

For centuries, it is customary for citizen's rights to differ from one region to the next, and to depend on a person's position in society. The end of the eighteenth century sees a growing awareness that every citizen should have the same rights, and that everybody exercising power should abide by the laws. In 1798, during the Batavian Republic (1795-1806), this is set down in the Constitution for the Batavian People. This is in fact the first Constitution of the Netherlands, which is why it is also referred to as the "Original Constitution". In 1815, during the reign of King William I, the Constitution for the Kingdom of the Netherlands is drafted; currently, it is still in force. Many ideas from the 1798 Constitution are reflected in the 1815 version.

1848

The Constitution has been subjected to several major revisions. In 1848, revolutions and riots break out in several European countries, including the Netherlands. This upsets King William II. He requests

liberal statesman Johan Rudolph Thorbecke to amend the Constitution to such effect as to curtail the power of the monarch and to accord more power to the Ministers and Parliament. With this amendment, Thorbecke lays the foundation for the parliamentary system and the further administrative structure of the country. Therefore, the "1848 Constitution" has come to be regarded as the beginnings of Dutch democracy.

Twentieth century

In 1917, male suffrage is introduced. Women are not entitled to vote but do become eligible for election. In 1919, they are enfranchised and by 1922, women can exercise their voting rights for the first time. After 1945, decolonisation prompts new revisions. In 1983, an overall revision follows, involving the addition of basic social rights and a general stipulation against discrimination. From then on, Article 1 reads: *All persons in the Netherlands shall be treated equally in equal circumstances. Discrimination on the grounds of religion, belief, political opinion, race or sex or on any other grounds whatsoever shall not be permitted*. Since 2010, attempts are being made to have Article 1 include the prohibition of discrimination on the grounds of "disability or sexual orientation", to reflect social consensus on such issues.

Such an amendment would tie in with earlier decrees, such as the introduction of same-sex marriages in 2001. By 2020, the proposition for this amendment to the Constitution is still under consideration. The Constitution is not as easily amendable as other Acts and the process takes a long time.

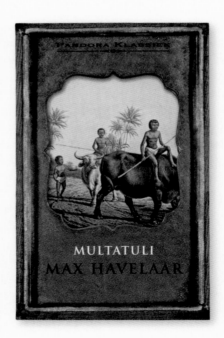

1860

Max Havelaar

Injustice in the Dutch East Indies

In his novel *Max Havelaar*, Multatuli criticises the government on account of the Dutch colonial administration. As an official in the Dutch East Indies, Multatuli witnesses how the Dutch are exploiting the local population. His novel becomes a best seller and feeds the resistance against colonialism.

Cultivation System

In 1859, a disappointed government official in the Dutch East Indies by the name of Eduard Douwes Dekker writes a literary novel under the pseudonym of Multatuli. The novel, entitled *Max Havelaar; or, the Coffee Auctions of the Dutch Trading Company*, is a fierce condemnation of the abuses under colonial rule in the Dutch East Indies. Such abuses are largely brought about by the so-called Cultivation System, a tax system introduced in 1830 by the Governor General of the Dutch East Indies, Johannes van den Bosch. He intends to have the financially malfunctioning colony become profitable for the Netherlands.

Under the Cultivation System, the population is forced to make a piece of land available for the cultivation of a set volume of products. These products, such as coffee, sugar, tea, and indigo dye, must subsequently be supplied to the Netherlands without any compensation. The system generates a great deal of money for the Netherlands, but it does not work out well for the locals. Exploitation and famine ensue. This provokes increasingly more criticism. One of these critics is Multatuli.

The story

Max Havelaar is published in 1860. It is a frame tale featuring several interwoven storylines. It begins with the tale of Batavus Droogstoppel, coffee broker and textbook example of a petty bourgeois, unimaginative, miserly man. He symbolises the Dutch exploitation of the colony. One day, Droogstoppel is visited by a former classmate, Sjaalman, who asks him to publish a manuscript.

What follows – interrupted by Droogstoppel's commentary – is the tale of the manuscript. The fictional character of Max Havelaar is roughly based on what the author, Eduard Douwes Dekker, has actually experienced as a government official in the Dutch East Indies. Max Havelaar speaks up for the oppressed population of Java, but is thwarted by his Dutch superiors and by local profiteers collaborating with the Dutch.

The Droogstoppel and Havelaar storylines are interwoven with several other stories, such as the famous tale of Saïdjah and Adinda. Underneath this moving love story lies a bitter attack against the exploitation and cruelties suffered by the population of Java. At the end of the book, Multatuli makes a passionate plea directly to King William III, who as head of state bears final responsibility for the abuses and corruption in the Dutch East Indies.

Reception

Initially, the novel meets with criticism, but its popularity quickly grows. *Max Havelaar* is even discussed in the House of Representatives. The novel ties in with a more comprehensive literary movement of nineteenth-century authors who use their work to speak up against injustice. For example, in *Max Havelaar*, Multatuli refers to the American writer Harriet Beecher Stowe, the author of the famous novel *Uncle Tom's Cabin*, which has stirred up public condemnation of slavery. A Dutch Cabinet Minister even calls Multatuli "the Dutch Beecher Stowe".

Max Havelaar is reprinted to this very day. Meanwhile, the book has been translated into dozens of languages. In 1999, in *The New York Times*, the Indonesian author Pramudya Ananta Tur referred to it as "The Book That Killed Colonialism".

The Child Protection Act of Van Houten

Out of the factory and into the school

Children are cheap workers, and consequently factory owners are keen on hiring them. As the number of factories increases, resistance against child labour grows. In 1874, the Child Protection Act initiated by politician Samuel van Houten prohibits labour by children up to the age of twelve. From 1901 onwards, all children aged seven to twelve must go to school.

Child labour

Throughout history, child labour has been a common phenomenon. Children work the fields, in shops or in workshops. This is not just regarded as useful – enabling them to learn a trade – but in many cases, it is a dire necessity to supplement the family income. During the Industrial Revolution, increasingly more children are put to work in factories, frequently under poor working conditions. A well-known case in point is the Petrus Regout glass factory in Maastricht, whose kilns burn day and night. The factory operates with two shifts, each working twelve hours at a stretch. Around midnight, children aged between eight and ten years old walk the streets half asleep to start their shift.

Criticism

From the early nineteenth century, legislation is introduced that somewhat curtails child labour. In 1839, such an Act is adopted in the German state of Prussia. Around 1860, child labour is increasingly criticised in the Netherlands. Physicians and teachers explain that the work performed by children jeopardises their health, and that children belong at school. Factory owners gradually come to realise that it would make more sense for them to hire children who have completed primary school. After all, children aged twelve and older, who can read and write, can be put to work in a wider range of factory jobs.

An important voice in the debate is that of author Jacob Jan Cremer. In 1863, after visiting a cloth factory in Leiden, he makes a burning plea to a select group of people gathered in The Hague. He sketches the horrible conditions under which children are forced to work and urges the King to abolish child labour with immediate effect. Among the shocked audience are several MPs and factory owners. Cremer's plea comes as a bombshell and it is published under the title of *Factory Children*. That same year, under the pressure of public opinion, Minister Thorbecke establishes a state committee to investigate child labour.

Legislation

In 1874, liberal politician Samuel van Houten submits a private member's bill against "excessive labour and neglect of children". This bill prohibits children up to the age of twelve from working in workshops and factories. Although Van Houten pursues a general ban, the House of Representatives mitigates his bill. For example, children are still allowed to do farm work. And a lack of supervisory bodies precludes the abolition of child labour in factories with immediate effect. The 1901 Compulsory Education Act ends child labour once and for all. From that time onwards, parents are obliged to send their children between the ages of seven up to and including twelve to school. In actual practice, most parents already do so. Around 1900, 90 per cent of children attend school.

Under the International Convention on the Rights of the Child (1989), child labour is currently prohibited if it is "unhealthy or harmful". Yet in 2019, as many as 152 million children across the globe are working, of whom 73 million under hazardous circumstances.

1853-1890

Vincent van Gogh

Painter in a new age

The story of his life is as colourful as many of his paintings.
In his lifetime, his radically innovative painting style is appreciated by
virtually no-one. As a result, he feels lonely and unrecognised.
Only after his suicide does he rise to fame; nowadays, his paintings
are admired by millions of people from all over the world.

Artist

Vincent van Gogh is born in 1853 in the village of Zundert, in the province of Brabant. At a young age, he already travels extensively across the Netherlands and Europe. After countless jobs and a failed attempt at university study, Van Gogh eventually opts for an existence as an artist. He takes painting lessons and draws a lot. In 1885, he paints his famous *The Potato Eaters* in Nuenen: a gloomy and dark portrait of a peasant family. This painting style and its theme – the life and suffering of ordinary people – are characteristic of Van Gogh's early work.

The following year, he moves to Paris, the city in which many people are engaged in the innovation of painting. His brother Theo is an art dealer here; he introduces Vincent to the paintings and drawings of the French Impressionists. These painters' use of light and colour is more refined than what Van Gogh is accustomed to. It inspires him to experiment: his work becomes more colourful and he starts to paint with the short brush strokes that will later become world famous. He also collects Japanese woodcuts, whose influence is reflected in his later work.

In 1888, Van Gogh rents a studio in the south of France: the "Yellow House" in Arles, made famous by his rendition of it. To his sister Wil he writes that the lavish natural beauty of the south calls for a new way of painting. "Distinctly colourful: sky blue, pink, orange, vermillion, bright yellow, bright green, bright wine red, violet". He often paints landscapes and because he cannot afford a model, he paints many self-portraits.

Illness and death

Vincent van Gogh's life is marked by upheaval, lost loves, and financial problems. He frequently quarrels with his artist friends. One day, a conflict gets out of hand and Vincent threatens fellow artist Paul Gauguin with a razor. Shortly afterwards, Van Gogh cuts off a piece of his own left ear, either accidentally or on purpose. Some of his self-portraits show him with a bandaged ear. Van Gogh is increasingly troubled by mental problems. For a while, he has himself committed to a psychiatric institution, in which he produces renowned paintings of cypresses and starry skies. On 27 July 1890, he walks into a corn field and shoots himself in the chest. He dies two days later.

World fame

His fame does not begin to grow until after his death. On the one hand, this can be attributed to his paintings, which are powerful, colourful, and unique. On the other hand, the story of his life excites wide interest: he is the textbook example of an artist who is as brilliant as he is lonely. Moreover, his work inspires many later painters.

Nowadays, Vincent van Gogh is world famous. Every year, the Van Gogh Museum in Amsterdam attracts some two million visitors, more than 80 per cent of whom come from abroad. His work is also on display in other museums, both within and beyond the Netherlands. The artist Vincent van Gogh is currently held in such great esteem that his work is worth a lot of money. In 2017, Christie's auctions his *Laboureur dans un champ* for nearly 70 million euros.

1854–1929

Aletta Jacobs

Standing up for equal rights

Aletta Jacobs is the first woman in Dutch history officially to be admitted to university. Furthermore, she is the first woman to become a physician and the first woman to earn a PhD. In the Netherlands, she is renowned as the leader of the first wave of feminism and on account of her crusade for female suffrage.

Childhood

Aletta Jacobs is born in Sappemeer, in the province of Groningen. In 1871, while in secondary school, she writes a letter to Minister Thorbecke requesting permission to be admitted to the "academic lessons". She wants to go to medical school. Thorbecke replies to her father that permission is granted. Therefore, a seventeen-year-old girl has been instrumental in opening up Dutch universities to women. To that date, only one exception has ever been made to male academic exclusivity: in 1636, Anna Maria van Schurman is allowed to attend lectures at the University of Utrecht, sitting behind a curtain so as not to distract the male students.

Physician

After earning her PhD, Jacobs moves to London, where she meets progressive female physicians. Later she sets up practice as a general practitioner on the Herengracht canal in Amsterdam, where she gives free consultations to women and provides them with contraceptives. The latter is quite revolutionary: at the time, little is known about birth control and many women are exhausted by their annual pregnancies. Furthermore, Jacobs calls attention to the physical ailments of shop girls, some of whom are forced to remain standing for eleven hours at a time. Her efforts result in the adoption of a bill that requires shops to provide their staff with "seating facilities".

Female suffrage

In 1889, Jacobs travels to London to attend a conference on female suffrage. This inspires her. When Wilhelmina Drucker founds the *Vereeniging voor Vrouwenkiesrecht* (Society for Women's Suffrage, VvVK) in 1893, Jacobs joins her. In 1903, she is elected president. At the time, only a portion of the male population of the Netherlands is allowed to vote. The electoral law does not even mention women. The prevailing opinion is that politics would keep them from their main duty: the family.

The Society for Women's Suffrage holds a different view and is fully committed to women's right to vote. The members organise exhibitions, publish newspapers and pamphlets, and submit petitions. In 1916, the society organises a demonstration for female suffrage which is attended by no fewer than 18,000 men and women. The crusade for suffrage has penetrated the entire country and is supported by rich and poor alike.

In 1917, men are universally enfranchised. Women only become eligible for election. The female suffrage bill devised by Jacobs is passed in 1919. In 1922, female suffrage is actually embedded in the Constitution: women now have the right to vote. At the time, Aletta Jacobs is 68 years old. In the Dutch colonies (Dutch East Indies, Surinam, and the Netherlands Antilles) female suffrage remains strictly limited until after World War II.

Women's Congress

Jacobs rises to international fame after organising the *International Women's Congress* in The Hague in 1915. 1100 women from twelve countries, including the belligerent nations, meet on neutral turf to speak about peace. They formulate proposals that are submitted to their heads of state. This leads Jacobs to visit the American President, Woodrow Wilson. Wilson's plea in 1918 for the establishment of an association of nations that together will keep the peace is remarkably similar to the recommendations of the Congress. In 1919, this results in the establishment of the League of Nations, a predecessor to the United Nations.

Women's lib

The biggest changes in the position of women take place during the twentieth century, in particular as a result of the "second wave of feminism". In the 1960s, the "Dolle Minas" (named after Wilhelmina Drucker) campaign for the liberation of women. They refuse to be condemned to the life of a housewife, like their mothers. In 1980, the "Equal Opportunities Act" is adopted.

1914–1918

World War I

Wartime neutrality

From 1914 to 1918, the "Great War" rages worldwide. Millions of civilians and soldiers are killed. The Netherlands is neutral, which saves the population from the worst horrors. The war impacts the country nonetheless: refugees pour in, food becomes scarce, and unemployment is high.

The Great War

World War I is the first major war involving millions of soldiers and civilians all across the globe. In this conflict, the "Central Powers" (Germany, Austria-Hungary, and the Ottoman Empire) oppose the "Allies" (France, Great Britain, and Russia). The war front is not limited to Europe, but extends to Africa, Asia, and the Middle East. Some of the warring countries possess many colonies. As a result, soldiers from all over the world are drafted to fight.

Combat in France and Belgium largely takes place from the infamous trenches that offer little protection to the soldiers. They are at great risk when having to leave the trenches to attack the enemy. Hundreds of thousands of soldiers lose their lives at the front. The Allies start to gain ground when the United States enters the war on their side in 1917. In November 1918, the Central Powers surrender. The war claims the lives of ten million soldiers and at least ten million civilians. Its disruptions may have exacerbated the deadliness of the Spanish Flu pandemic, which in 1918 and 1919 kills 50 million people worldwide and nearly 40,000 people in the Netherlands.

Neutrality

Immediately after the outbreak of World War I, the Netherlands declares its neutrality. The Netherlands is but a small country and its army is no match for that of such neighbouring countries as England and Germany. Furthermore, the Netherlands is afraid of losing its colonies in a war. That is why the Netherlands and Belgium choose to remain neutral, as they have been for decades. The Belgian effort is thwarted, because the German army invades the country in order quickly to advance towards Paris. The Netherlands is more fortunate and manages to maintain its neutrality, as do, e.g., Denmark, Spain, and Switzerland. The Dutch success in remaining neutral can mainly be attributed to the fact that this benefits both England and Germany: to them, the Netherlands serves as a buffer zone.

Neutrality turns out to be a position that is difficult to sustain. At the beginning of the war, more than a million Belgians flee to the Netherlands. Encampments are erected to take in the refugees. Among them are many war volunteers who wish to join the Allies. The Germans subsequently construct a 332-km stretch of lethal electric fencing between the Netherlands and Belgium. The barrier will come to be known as the "Wire of Death".

Great Britain blockades trade with Germany and prohibits the Netherlands from selling imported products to the Germans. The Germans, on the other hand, attempt to collect as many foodstuffs and raw materials from the Netherlands as they can. Three hundred Dutch ships perish after being hit by British mines or German torpedoes. Unemployment soars as international trade diminishes. Food becomes scarce and is rationed. In 1917 and 1918, food supplies in Amsterdam and Rotterdam are plundered by desperate housewives.

Revolution

By the end of the war, several European countries are in revolutionary mood. In Russia, the Czar is deposed and murdered. After the war, the German Emperor flees to the Netherlands, whereupon Germany becomes a republic. The Netherlands also perceives the threat of revolution, which prompts the government to make far-reaching promises in order to settle the political upheaval, such as the eight-hour working day and general suffrage (1919).

1898 – 1945

Anton de Kom

Fighting racism and colonialism

Anton de Kom is a Surinamese anti-colonial writer, activist, and resistance hero. In 1934, he publishes his book entitled *Wij slaven van Suriname* [We Slaves of Surinam], an indictment of racism, exploitation, and colonial oppression. It is still widely read, because it allows a broad public insight into colonial power structures.

Surinam

Anton de Kom is born in Paramaribo, the capital of Surinam, at that time a Dutch colony. His father was born a slave on the Molhoop plantation, just before slavery was abolished in 1863. Anton earns a bookkeeping diploma in Surinam, but racist policy prevents him from landing a good job. He leaves for the Netherlands to try his luck there.

The Netherlands

In 1921, De Kom arrives in the Netherlands. In The Hague he finds employment with a coffee and tea merchant. Here, he meets Petronella Borsboom. They marry in 1926. Such a mixed marriage is regarded as unusual in the predominantly white country of that time. Anton and Nel have four children.

In addition to his work, Anton develops into a writer and poet. Dissatisfied with the lack of knowledge in the Netherlands about the history of Surinam and its slavery past, he starts giving lectures on the topic. Inspired by the fight against racism in the United States and the equality ideals of communist organisations in the Netherlands, he publishes critical political essays. He befriends communists and feels an affinity with Indonesian students pursuing the independence of the Dutch East Indies.

By the end of 1932, he and his family leave for Surinam to visit his dying mother. Back in Surinam, he continues his political activities. His lectures are banned by the authorities. Anton establishes a consultancy. Many Surinamese from various ethnic backgrounds come to him for advice and before long he is dubbed "Papa De Kom". In fear of the resistance that De Kom is stirring up with his activities, he is imprisoned by the authorities. On 7 February 1933, a huge crowd assembles in front of the prison to pledge their support for De Kom. Soldiers open fire, killing two and wounding 22 protesters. In order to prevent further insurrection, De Kom is exiled from Surinam and forced to return to the Netherlands.

We Slaves of Surinam

In the Netherlands, he fails to find further employment. However, he continues to write. In 1934, he publishes his work *We Slaves of Surinam*, the first history book about Surinam written by a Surinamese author. The final chapter of his book deals with his exile. De Kom's work ties in with a timeframe that sees more international anti-colonial and anti-racist works, such as *The Black Jacobins* by C.L.R. James. The famous final sentences of *We Slaves of Surinam* read:

> "Sranang my fatherland.
> Once I hope to see you again.
> On the day when all misery
> shall be erased from you."

World War II

However, De Kom would not see Surinam again. During the German occupation of the Netherlands, he joins the resistance. On 7 August 1944, he is arrested by the occupying forces, on account of the articles he writes for *De Vonk*, an illegal communist journal in The Hague. Via several camps, he eventually ends up in Sandbostel concentration camp, where he dies on 24 April 1945. His body, buried in a mass grave, is not identified until 1960.

In the 1960s, university students rediscover his book. Following the independence of Surinam in 1975, De Kom is increasingly hailed as a hero. His books and his mental legacy still serve as a source of inspiration, both in the Netherlands and in Surinam.

1940-1945

World War II

The Netherlands occupied and liberated

On 10 May 1940, the German army invades the Netherlands. During the occupation, more than a hundred thousand Dutch Jews are killed in concentration camps. Some Dutch citizens protest, but most of them are passively anti-German.

Adolf Hitler

In 1933, Adolf Hitler comes to power in Germany as the leader of the right extremist National Socialist German Workers Party (NSDAP). This party, whose adherents are referred to as Nazis, grows as a result of the economic crisis and the feelings of revenge for the way in which Germany has been treated after World War I. Hitler intends to make Germany the most powerful country in Europe. In 1938, he seizes his native country, Austria. Subsequently, he annexes part of Czechoslovakia. Upon his invasion of Poland, Britain and France declare war on Nazi Germany: the war has commenced. In May 1940, Hitler attacks France, concurrently occupying the Netherlands and Belgium.

On the morning of Friday, 10 May 1940, German soldiers cross the Dutch border. The Dutch army is no match for the German war machine. After the Germans bomb the centre of Rotterdam, the Dutch military command decides to surrender. By then, the government and the Queen have already departed for England.

Occupation

Initially, the Dutch occupied territory is ruled by the German army, but before long, Hitler appoints a civilian administration. He has his reasons: to him, the Dutch constitute a "Germanic brother people" to be won over to national socialism. In his opinion, the best way to achieve this goal is to leave the administration to the Dutch wherever possible, with an upper tier of German officials. The Germans are assisted by members of the National Socialist Movement (NSB), a Dutch party holding views similar to those of the German NSDAP, and aided by hangers-on and profiteers.

When Hitler launches an attack against the Soviet Union in 1941, some twenty thousand Dutch men join the German army. Others, however, join the resistance. They publish their own newspapers that are secretly distributed. In addition, they assault German occupiers and Nazi collaborators. Towards the end of the war, the resistance movement garners increasing support. However, a majority of the Dutch population is passively anti-German and adapts to the circumstances.

Persecution

Initially, the occupation seems not so bad, but the population quickly finds out what the absence of freedom entails. The occupying forces respond to the first acts of resistance with severe punishments. Dutch men are forced to work in German factories. People are locked up in prisons and concentration camps without any form of due process. For the Dutch Jews, life becomes particularly difficult as a result of the growing number of anti-Jewish measures. From 1942 onwards, the German occupying forces deport more than a hundred thousand Jewish men, women, and children from the Netherlands, cramming them into freight trains to be transported to concentration camps. An overwhelming majority are murdered. Under the Nazi reign of terror, an estimated six million Jews and hundreds of thousands of Sinti, Roma, disabled people, homosexuals, and Jehovah's witnesses are killed.

Winter of starvation and liberation

In the autumn of 1944, the southern part of the Netherlands is liberated by Allied forces. The liberation of the area north of the major rivers does not start until the spring of 1945. In the intervening months, the western provinces still have to endure the "Winter of Starvation", which hits the cities particularly hard. Estimates are that at least twenty thousand people die for lack of food.
On 5 May 1945, the German army surrenders, and the Netherlands is liberated. At this time, the Dutch East Indies are still occupied by the Japanese. Following the nuclear attacks on Hiroshima and Nagasaki, Japan capitulates on 15 August 1945.

Commemoration

The memories of this traumatic war continue to exert a powerful influence on Dutch society. The war casualties are commemorated every year on 4 May, whilst the liberation is celebrated annually on 5 May.

1929–1945

Anne Frank

The persecution of the Jews

During the German occupation, Anne Frank goes into hiding in the secret annex of an Amsterdam canalside house, along with her family and four others. In 1944, they are discovered, and eventually Anne dies in a concentration camp. After the war, her diary is published. It becomes one of the most widely read books in the world. Thus, Anne Frank puts a face to the victims of the Holocaust.

From Germany to Amsterdam

Anne Frank is born in 1929 into a Jewish family in the German city of Frankfurt am Main. After Adolf Hitler seizes power in 1933, the family flees to Amsterdam to escape the growing anti-Semitism. Hitler regards Jews as a dangerous and inferior race that does not belong in his empire. Between 1933 and 1937, some 140,000 Jews flee from Germany, some 35,000 of whom end up in the Netherlands for a period of time. The Frank family finds a home in the Rivierenbuurt district of Amsterdam.

Anne goes to school there, learns Dutch, and makes new friends.

Anti-Jewish measures

Having occupied the Netherlands in May 1940, Nazi Germany is quick to take measures aimed at separating the Jews from the rest of the population. Anne is transferred to a Jewish school. Cinemas, cafés, markets, theatres, and parks are marked with signs stating, "No Jews allowed". From May 1942 onwards, Jews are required to wear a yellow Star of David, in order to be recognisable in public. That summer, the German occupying forces in the Netherlands launch a major operation intended to transport the Jews to Eastern Europe. Jewish families are notified to pack their bags to work in the East. They are taken from their homes and put on a train to Westerbork transit camp in the province of Drenthe. From there, they are transported to concentration and extermination camps elsewhere in Europe.

Into hiding

The Frank family starts looking for a safe-house. Along with four other people, they hide in some concealed rooms behind a book-case in the building where Anne's father Otto Frank works, on the Prinsengracht canal in Amsterdam. There, Anne begins writing the diary that would bring her fame after the war. As a young, ambitious girl, she writes about what she experiences in the secret annex. Writing is a way of release for her, a way to persevere in the stifling hiding place. For two years, the family manages to stay hidden. Until they are arrested on 4 August 1944, possibly after having been betrayed.

Persecution

Via Westerbork transit camp, the Franks are transported to Auschwitz-Birkenau extermination camp. A few months later, Anne and her sister Margot are deported once more, to Bergen-Belsen concentration camp. Here, the sisters succumb to typhus in 1945. Their mother Edith Frank dies in Auschwitz. Otto Frank is the only one of the family to survive the war.

A total of more than a hundred thousand Dutch Jews are murdered in the various concentration and extermination camps. Compared to the rest of Europe, a proportionally large number of Jews have been deported from the Netherlands. Between 1933 and 1945, some six million Jews and hundreds of thousands of persecuted individuals – among whom are Sinti and Roma, disabled people, homosexuals, and Jehovah's witnesses – are killed by the Nazis.

World fame

After the war, Miep Gies, who has been helping the family while they were in hiding, hands Otto Frank a stack of notebooks: the diaries of his daughter Anne. In 1947, the diary is published in the Netherlands under the title of *Het Achterhuis*. The English language translation – *Anne Frank: The Diary of a Young Girl* – appears in 1952. It gains worldwide fame after an American stage adaptation in 1955, just in time to save the actual building, that was due for demolition. This same building, which nowadays is called the Anne Frank House, is currently visited by more than a million people a year, from all over the world.

![Proklamasi handwritten declaration]

1945-1949

Indonesia

The struggle for independence

Shortly after World War II, Dutch troops are dispatched to the recently proclaimed Republic of Indonesia to restore the old rule. In spite of the ensuing war, involving a great deal of violence, Indonesia remains independent. In 1949, this independence is acknowledged by the Netherlands.

Independence

'Proklamasi. Kami bangsa Indonesia dengan ini menjatakan kemerdekaan Indonesia...'
'We, the people of Indonesia, hereby declare that Indonesia is independent...'

This is how Sukarno informed the world, in Jakarta on 17 August 1945, that the colonial Dutch East Indies definitively belonged to the past. Two days earlier, Japan had surrendered, following the atomic bombs on the Japanese cities of Hiroshima and Nagasaki. This marked the end of World War II in Asia.

Even before the war, the Dutch East Indies harboured a comprehensive activist movement that advocated the right to self-determination. Leaders such as Sukarno, Mohammad Hatta, and Sutan Sjahrir pursue full independence, whilst others aim for increased autonomy. However, the Dutch authorities remain firmly in control. And then, in 1942, Japan invades the Dutch East Indies. On 27 February, the allied forces lose the Battle of the Java Sea and capitulation follows on 8 March. Soldiers are made prisoners of war and held captive under terrible circumstances. Dutch residents and later on, also Dutch residents of Indonesian descent, are detained in horrible camps. The administrative system of the Dutch East Indies is rendered inoperative by the Japanese and in effect, the Dutch East Indies cease to exist.

War of Independence

The Netherlands does not acknowledge the Republic of Indonesia. From 1945 onwards, it resorts to negotiations, warfare, and violence in an attempt to restore its rule, or at least stay in control of the decolonisation process. More than 200,000 troops partake in this war, over half of whom are conscripts. The largest military operations of the Netherlands are Operation Product in 1947 and Operation Crow in 1948-1949. During the latter, Sukarno is imprisoned. The two operations are referred to as "police actions". The United Nations orders the Dutch to cease the military actions and to release the prisoners. The Netherlands does not cave in to the international pressure until May 1949. On the Indonesian side, more than 100,000 are killed during the period 1945-1949, versus some 5,000 on the Dutch side. On 27 December 1949, the transfer of sovereignty is signed in Amsterdam.

New Guinea is the only territory that is not relinquished until 1962. After a transitional period under UN supervision, the region is transferred to Indonesia in 1963, without taking account of the wishes of the Papua population. The state borders of the current Republic of Indonesia thus coincide with those of the former Dutch East Indies.

Migration

On account of the new balance of power, a total of more than 300,000 Dutch nationals, Dutch residents of Indonesian descent, and members of Indonesian minority groups (Moluccans, Papuans, Chinese) leave the country well into the 1960s. Most of them head for the Netherlands, among whom are 12,500 Moluccan soldiers of the former Royal Netherlands East Indies Army (KNIL) and their families. They are promised a free Moluccan state to which they can return. However, this promise is never redeemed. In the 1970s, this results in shocking hijackings by young Moluccan activists.

Not a thing of the past

For a long period of time, the lost colonial war is hushed up. The views of the large group of veterans and a diverse group of migrants from the former colony differ widely. In 2008, the recognition of the war crimes is taken to court. A well-known example is the Rawagede case. In 1947, 431 men in the village of Rawagede in West Java were shot by Dutch troops. Some sixty years later, their widows sued the Dutch state for damages. In 2011, the court ruled that the widows are entitled to such compensation.

The Netherlands still struggles with the recognition of Sukarno's proclamation and the subsequent war. In 2020, 75 years after the Proklamasi, King Willem-Alexander apologises for "excessive violence" during the war and congratulates Indonesia on 75 years of independence.

1953

The Great Flood

The danger of water

The Delta Works are renowned across the globe. They have been constructed
to prevent a catastrophic flood like the one that hit in 1953.
In that disastrous night, the dykes of the southwestern part of
the Netherlands give way to a violent storm surge. 200,000 hectares
of land are flooded, and 1836 people lose their lives.

The disastrous night of 1953

In the night of 31 January - 1 February 1953,
a severe storm surge hits Zeeland, West-
Brabant, and the South Holland islands.
Many dykes burst. The icy cold water has a
devastating impact: 200,000 hectares of land
are flooded, 1836 people lose their lives, tens

of thousands of animals drown, and 72,000
are left homeless. It is a national disaster.

Immediate action along the Hollandse IJssel
river manages to prevent a far worse disaster.
When the dyke near Nieuwerkerk aan den

IJssel starts to give way, a ship is navigated into the breach, and as a result, the dyke holds. Behind this dyke lies the lowest part of the Netherlands, some of which is situated up to seven metres below sea level. The area accommodates more than a million people.

All over the Netherlands, clothing and money is collected. Evacuees are warmly welcomed, and aid also arrives from abroad. For example, a large number of wooden emergency houses are donated for families left homeless. Closing all the dykes that have burst takes until the end of 1953.

The Delta Works

As early as the 1930s, hydraulic engineer Johan van Veen warns about a disastrous flood, but virtually no-one listens. The existing plans for coastal reinforcement are continuously put on hold, on account of World War II and the post-war reconstruction. Towards the end of January 1953, Van Veen submits his Delta Plan to his superiors at the Ministry of Public Works. A few days later, the dykes give way.

After the disaster, the authorities are quick to start implementing Van Veen's plans: a system comprising several dams and flood defences to protect the southwestern part of the Netherlands against flooding. A storm surge barrier is created on the Hollandse IJssel river. All the tidal inlets between the South Holland and Zeeland islands are closed off by dams, except for the Westerschelde. The sea and river dykes are improved. This pioneering project is one of the most sophisticated hydraulic achievements in the world. Its masterpiece is the closable storm surge barrier in the Oosterschelde, which was put into operation in 1986.

This huge project provides the southwest of the Netherlands with far better flood protection. At the same time, new dams and dykes improve access to the Zeeland islands – which boosts the development of industry and tourism in this province.

Room for the river

The 1953 disaster demonstrates how vulnerable large parts of the Netherlands are to waterlogging and flooding. The sea is not the only body of water to pose a threat: rivers can also flood. Climate change is contributing to substantial fluctuations in precipitation across Europe, which affects the water levels of the major rivers.

In 1993 and 1995, the rivers Rhine, Waal, and Meuse reach dangerously high water levels. In 1995, as a precautionary measure, 250,000 people and a million animals are evacuated from the area around the major rivers. It is a narrow escape. In the province of Limburg, on the other hand, the undyked villages of Borgharen and Itteren are flooded. These near-disasters prompt a turning point in water management. Whereas in the past, rivers used to be increasingly contained by dykes, at the beginning of this century they are given more room at crucial locations.

The future

Meanwhile, it is clear that the rising sea level and extreme waterlogging have long ceased to be issues that solely affect the Netherlands. As a result of climate change, these issues have become an international challenge.

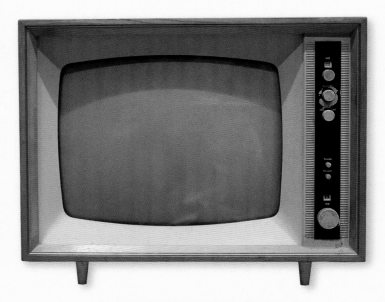

from 1948 onwards

Television

The world on your screen

Television brings the world closer. In 1948, Philips introduces the television set in the Netherlands and by around 1970, virtually every family has one. The TV offers entertainment, but some programmes provoke heated discussion.

Radio and "pillarisation"

The development of the television is pursued as early as in 1880, but it takes another seventy years for the device to end up in living rooms. The radio arrives earlier: the first device that enables people to bring news, music, and entertainment directly into their own homes. From 1920 onwards, radio broadcasting services such as AVRO, NCRV, KRO, VARA, and VPRO are set up at a rapid pace.

The Netherlands is divided into groups, referred to as "pillars". Each pillar is associated with a particular political party, trade union, newspaper, and now also a particular radio service. Broadcasting times are divided among the services, and each is free to decide on its broadcasts which are aimed at its own pillar. In this respect, the Dutch broadcasting system differs from that of, e.g., the United Kingdom, in which a national entity – the BBC – aims to serve all of society.

First official broadcast
In the Netherlands, the Eindhoven-based company Philips is the driving force behind the introduction of television. In 1948, Philips starts to experiment with TV broadcasts that can only be received in and around Eindhoven. In 1951, the radio services take over from Philips. Together, they establish the *Nederlandse Televisie Stichting* [Dutch Television Foundation, NTS]. On 2 October 1951, the NTS stages its first official national broadcast. Later on, the NTS is re-named NOS [Dutch Broadcast Foundation].

It does not take long for the Dutch to start watching programmes other than those intended for their own group. Some programmes are so popular that people associated with other pillars enjoy watching them too. Examples of such cross-pillar programmes are *Swiebertje* (NCRV, from 1955 onwards) and *Pipo de Clown* (VARA, from 1958 onwards). Another unifying programme is the fund-raising campaign *Open het Dorp* [Open the Village]. This AVRO programme, hosted by Dutch TV icon Mies Bouwman, is broadcast simultaneously on radio and television in 1962; it lasts 23 hours. A sum of more than twelve million guilders is collected in the purview of a health care institution for disabled people in Arnhem.

Watching at the neighbour's
In the 1950s, the first TV sets feature a small black-and-white screen and are very expensive. Only some five hundred Dutch residents can afford to buy one. In those early years, it is quite common for people to watch TV together with neighbours or friends who already own a set. The sale of television sets soars. By around 1970, a black-and-white television set is found in virtually every home; some even own a colour TV.

By then, the average Dutch person spends about an hour and a half watching TV. Critics argue that watching TV encourages passivity and consumerism. However, the advocates point out that the new medium brings families together – joined in front of the TV – and has an informative function.

Whatever the case may be, television plays an important role in the formation of opinions regarding societal topics. Because of the limited choice (up until 1964, only one channel and up until 1988, just two), many people watch the same programmes. Newscasts, drama, entertainment, and sports attract a wide audience. Programmes focused on controversial topics such as sex, women's liberation, youth culture, religion, and the royal family elicit a great deal of discussion.

The Internet
The introduction of cable TV, satellites, and the Internet has greatly expanded and globalised the range of television programmes. Compared to 1970, nowadays most people tend to spend many more hours in front of a screen, whilst watching TV as a family activity is losing ground, because everyone can receive the world on his or her own smartphone or tablet. Philosopher Marshall McLuhan already predicted this in 1959: the world has become a village, a "global village". Television and the Internet have been instrumental in this development.

from c. 1880 onwards

The Port of Rotterdam

Gateway to the world

In the Rotterdam port area, goods from all over the world enter
the Netherlands, subsequently to be conveyed to the European hinterland.
The port is situated in the Rhine and Meuse delta, and accessible to
ocean-going vessels. Trade accounts for a large proportion of
the Dutch national income and Rotterdam constitutes the main hub.

Dam in the River Rotte

Rotterdam does not start to develop into
the main port of the Netherlands until the
nineteenth century. At the time, its port has
already existed for centuries. By around the
year 1250, a dam is constructed in the estuary
of the Rotte peat river. At this dam, freight is
transferred from river boats onto coasters:
these are the beginnings of the Port of
Rotterdam. In the sixteenth century,
Rotterdam develops into a major fishing port.
Although the city is subsequently involved
in colonial expeditions, Rotterdam never

becomes the centre of colonial trade: the port is silted up, which obstructs its access from the sea. Furthermore, the main financiers and entrepreneurs are located in Amsterdam.

In the second half of the nineteenth century, the port is expanded ever further, especially with a view to profiting from the emerging industry in the German Ruhr area. Under the direction of hydraulic engineer Pieter Caland (1826-1902), the dunes near Hoek van Holland are cut and a new connection to the port is dug. This Nieuwe Waterweg [New Waterway] vastly improves access to Rotterdam from the sea. In the actual port, new port basins are constructed. Machinery such as steam cranes enables more efficient loading and unloading. Inland vessels, trucks, and freight trains transport products at greater speeds.

Post-war reconstruction and expansion

During World War II, bombing severely damages nearly half of the port. Restoration of the Port of Rotterdam is given top priority in the post-war reconstruction of the Netherlands. Subsequently, the port grows at a rapid pace, in part as a result of the reviving trade with Germany. In the 1950s, expansion is already in order: the Eemhaven and Botlek areas date from those days. In 1962, the Port of Rotterdam becomes the largest port in the world. The Europoort area is completed in 1964, and in 1966, the first cargo container is unloaded in Rotterdam. In these huge, steel containers, break bulk cargo can be transported simply and safely, which enables large-scale loading and unloading. The port continues to grow: the Maasvlakte I and Maasvlakte II extensions are completed in 1973 and 2013.

New challenges

As a result of globalisation, worldwide freight transport is increasing. This means that competition is also growing: in 2004, Rotterdam loses its status as the world's largest port. The Dutch government sets great store by maintaining Rotterdam's competitive position, because the port is a key hub in the foreign trade network. In 2007, the Betuwe Route is opened, a railway line solely intended for freight transport between Rotterdam and Germany.

However, this unrestrained growth also raises a wide range of questions and protests. People are concerned about the port's role in diverting drugs, about safety risks, and about the impact that the expanded port area has on the natural environment. In addition to the economic impact of the growing port, another issue is how the port can be future-proofed.

1912–1986

Marga Klompé

The welfare state

In 1967, she has the opportunity to become the Netherlands'
first female Prime Minister, but in her opinion the country is not yet ready.
Marga Klompé is one of the key architects of the Dutch welfare state.
The General Social Assistance Act of 1965, warranting a livelihood
for all Dutch residents, can be credited to her.

First female minister

Marga Klompé is born in Arnhem, in a Roman Catholic family that is rather poorly off. On account of her talents, she is the only one of the five children to be allowed to continue her education; she earns a PhD in mathematics and physics. During World War II she is active as a courier for the resistance. When Arnhem is under attack in 1944, she coordinates the provision of medical care and food aid to many civilian refugees. She is also involved in the evacuation of the city. After its liberation, she assists in getting public life back on its feet.

Immediately after the war, she engages in politics. It annoys her that her party, the Catholic People's Party (KVP) does not have any female representatives in Parliament. In 1948, she is elected to the House of Representatives and in 1952, she becomes the first female MP for the European Coal and Steel Community, the predecessor to the European Union. In 1956, she becomes the first female Cabinet Minister in Dutch history. She is responsible for the Social Work portfolio in the Drees IV Cabinet.

Welfare state

In the successive Drees Cabinets (1948-1958), several important Acts are passed. Everyone aged 65 and over receives an old-age pension. MP Corry Tendeloo plays a key role in the abolition of the legal incompetence regulation, which means that from now on, married women do not require their husbands' permission to take decisions on money matters, work, and parenting. In the Netherlands, many extensions of the welfare state are not substantiated until the 1960s – i.e., later than in most other western European countries – when prosperity grows, and the government has more money to spend.

Klompé is one of the key driving forces behind this development. Many Dutch senior citizens live in "rest homes", in poor conditions. Klompé initiates an Act setting out strict regulations for such homes. Furthermore, in 1965 she introduces the General Social Assistance Act (ABW). Up until then, citizens who are unable to properly support themselves are assisted by welfare organisations or by family members. In Klompé's opinion, the government needs to intervene, if the assistance provided is insufficient. The Social Assistance Act provides for supplementary government benefits. Under the Act, social security becomes a right rather than charity. Living independently thus becomes easier for Dutch residents who are less well off.

Final years

When a new Cabinet is to be formed in 1967, Klompé's name is put forward by her party as a potential new Premier. She respectfully declines. In her view, the country is "not ripe yet" for a female Prime Minister. From 1967 until 1971, in the De Jong Cabinet, she once again holds a post as Minister. During these revolutionary times, she has a sympathetic ear for activists who pursue rapid changes in society. In 1971, Marga Klompé is the first woman to be appointed Minister of State: an honorary title bestowed by the Head of State to former politicians for exceptional merits in the governmental domain. She thus terminates her political career in order to devote herself fully to the Roman Catholic church. In spite of the serious illness from which she has been suffering since the 1980s, she continues her work insofar as her condition permits, until her death in 1986.

Legacy

The basis of the welfare state co-developed by Marga Klompé continues to underpin the Dutch social security system. Like other western European countries, in the 1980s the Netherlands starts to cut back on welfare provisions. Eventually, the General Social Assistance Act is replaced. The government now demands active participation in employment or education from citizens in order for them to qualify for benefits. Thus, the welfare state continues to evolve.

The immigrant workers

New Dutch residents

In the 1960s, the Dutch economy works overtime and the demand for workers is growing immensely. People from Spain, Portugal, Greece, the former Yugoslavia, Turkey, and Morocco are brought in to fill the gaps. They are referred to as "guest workers" because their presence will be temporary.

Economic growth

The exodus of Dutch nationals in the 1950s is the largest in Dutch history. Some 350,000 people emigrate with government support to countries such as Canada, New Zealand, and Australia. In the early 1960s, rapid economic growth sets in and, all of a sudden, the Netherlands needs all the workers it can get. Demand is particularly great in the manufacturing industries. For that reason, companies such as the Hoogovens steelworks and Philips start to look abroad. Employers want temporary workers, hence the name "guest workers".

Most of the initial workers to arrive in the Netherlands come from Italy, Spain, Greece, and Yugoslavia. Most of them are men. A recruitment agreement with Turkey in 1964 prompts Turkish workers to take their lead and five years later, Moroccan workers follow suit. In some cases, the Dutch government sends an "inspection committee" to collect workers in Morocco. A majority of the migrants live and work in the industrial hubs, such as the Port of Rotterdam and the textile region in the eastern part of the country. Many of them do heavy labour, put in long hours, and live under frugal circumstances.

From temporary to permanent

In the early years, the new labour forces are welcomed with open arms. After a while, however, some of the local populations make it quite clear that their presence is not appreciated. The government does not encourage them to settle down: the idea is that the workers will only be here for a limited period of time. In actual practice, things turn out differently. Employers continue to extend contracts until the recruitment of migrant workers is officially terminated in the 1970s, when manufacturing industry starts to decline. In the 1980s, the impact of the shrinking world economy is felt particularly strongly among these groups. Many workers remain in the Netherlands, especially when the Family Reunification Act (1974) opens up the possibility to send for their families.

From the 1980s onwards, the Dutch government has been working on an integration policy that continues to this day. Must newcomers adapt and blend into the majority culture, or can integration be achieved whilst retaining one's own identity? Or is integration a combination of these two views?

The multi-cultural society

With the arrival of this large group of workers, the Netherlands has once more become an immigration country. Apart from the influx of immigrant workers, the Netherlands grants asylum to political refugees, as do many other European countries. In addition, migrants from Surinam and the Antilles also settle in the Netherlands. Within the European Union, the Netherlands eliminates its borders, resulting in the immigration of workers from eastern Europe.

The various migration flows give rise to a heated political debate on the relationship between society, culture, and religion. This debate is exacerbated by the terrorist attacks of 11 September 2001 in the United States. A key issue is the position of Islam in Dutch society. A recurrent question in this respect is what exactly "Dutch citizenship" entails, and to what extent the Netherlands is receptive to newcomers.

Apart from the societal discussion, migrant children are prone to an accelerated individualisation process. Such children are found in all walks of life. Yet poor socio-economic conditions hamper many migrants in successfully moving up in society, whilst many of them are faced with discrimination in terms of participation in the labour market.

Children of immigrant workers are investigating how their parents' migration is impacting on their life. In 2018, Murat Isik wins the Libris Literature Award with his novel *Wees onzichtbaar* [Be Invisible], in which he tells the migration story of his Turkish family in southeast Amsterdam. Such a coming of age account gives this generation a sense of belonging and fosters connection.

1911-1995

Annie M.G. Schmidt

Going against the grain of a bourgeois country

"Never do what your mother tells you to do, then everything will be all right,"
to quote Annie M.G. Schmidt. Just saying what you want to say,
not making a fuss, breaking any rules that don't make sense,
and recalcitrant humour; these are the secrets of her pen.

Oeuvre

Annie M.G. Schmidt is born in 1911, the daughter of a clergyman on the Zuid-Beveland peninsula. She is a precocious child who views the world around her with curiosity. At the age of fourteen, she publishes her first rhyme. After World War II, she lands a job at the Amsterdam newspaper *Het Parool*, where she meets illustrator Fiep Westendorp.

From 1952 to 1957, the two of them produce a series of children's stories about a boy and a girl, Jip and Janneke. One of these stories is printed in the paper every day. This marks the beginning of a lifelong collaboration, resulting in illustrated children's novels such as *Pluk van de Petteflet* [which has been translated into English under the title

Tow-Truck Pluck] and *Minoes* [which served as the basis for the film entitled *Undercover Kitty*].

Schmidt's writings are quite diverse: in addition to columns, rhymes, poems, and children's stories, she also writes commentaries and cartoons. She makes up characters who speak their mind and go their own way. The characters have a wide range of friends, many of whom are children she would have wanted to be. With "Zebra Flopje" who is tired of those same old stripes and wants a different pair of PJs, and kings who do not like the food they are being served, she opposes rules, taboos, and prevailing standards.

Exponent of the spirit of the age

In the 1950s, Annie M.G. Schmidt is the creative force behind an immensely successful radio series, entitled *In Holland staat een huis* [About a house in Holland]. The radio play is broadcast twice a month and revolves around the Doorsnee family [the Average Family]. It paints a humorous picture of everyday life after the war. The series appeals to a wide audience and becomes very popular – which is unique in such a highly compartmentalised country as the Netherlands of the time.

Annie's work reflects events and frustrations from her own life, such as her lonely childhood and disappointments in love, but also tackles taboo subjects such as an affair with a married man and abortion. She writes cabaret lyrics and pioneering musicals, such as *Heerlijk duurt het langst* and *Foxtrot*, dealing with the liberation of women and homosexuals.

With her rebellious texts, Annie M.G. Schmidt is a highly influential yet gentle critic of the respectable, bourgeois, and "pillarised" nation. She herself does not escape criticism either. During the second wave of feminism in the 1970s, the feminists consider Jip and Janneke too role-reinforcing and old-fashioned. In the United States, the storybook characters run up against entirely different obstacles: the American publishers object to the fact that the illustrations picture the duo as all black silhouettes.

Children's literature

The work of Annie M.G. Schmidt ties in with a rich tradition of Dutch children's literature, which initially features many paragons of virtue, such as the hero of the poem "*Jantje zag eens pruimen hangen*" (1778) by Hiëronymus van Alphen. From the end of the nineteenth century onwards the scope widens, and children are allowed to be naughty. Well-known examples are *Dik Trom* (1891) by Johannes Kieviet and *Pietje Bell* (1914) by Chris van Abcoude. But naughty girls do not make their entry into children's books until after World War II, spurred on by *Pippi Longstocking* (1945) by the Swedish author Astrid Lindgren. Schmidt follows that track, for example, in *Floddertje*. In her stories, rebellious children often play a key role, which makes her immensely popular among both children and adults. Millions of copies of *Jip and Janneke* alone are sold, and her writings are translated into numerous languages. She is the recipient of many awards, among which are the *Zilveren Griffel* and the *Gouden Griffel* [the Silver Stylus and the Golden Stylus, respectively]. The *Gouden Griffel* is awarded annually to the best Dutch children's book; the *Zilveren Griffel* is awarded to the runner-up. The secret of her success? "I have always been eight years old. And I actually write for myself. I think that is the whole point. I am eight years old."

1974-2022?

Coal and gas

The energy issue

On 31 December 1974, the mines in Limburg close once and for all.
The last tub of coal leaves the Oranje-Nassau I mine near Heerlen,
the very last lift with miners comes up. The Netherlands pins its hopes
on another source of energy: natural gas.

Coal

How do I heat my home and my food?
For thousands of years, wood and peat were
the most commonly used fuels in the Low
Countries. Not until the nineteenth century
are they replaced by coal. This fossil fuel can
be mined in large volumes and is cheaper to
produce. Moreover, coal is the fuel used in the

purview of industrialisation: steam engines
run on coal. Coal gets the trains moving.

From 1900 onwards, coal extraction creates
new job opportunities in the Netherlands,
particularly in the province of Limburg,
where twelve mines are opened. For decades,

mining is a reliable source of employment. It attracts migrants and workers from far and wide, as far away as the Mediterranean. Towns such as Heerlen and Geleen evolve into prosperous, modern cities and are proud of their new facilities, such as hospitals and schools.

Closing the mines

And then the energy landscape changes. In 1959, giant gas reserves are discovered underneath the land of farmer Boon in Slochteren. This gas can easily be pumped up, and through a pipe grid it eventually ends up in virtually every home, where it is used to fuel gas heaters and stoves. Coal still remains important for the industry, but abroad its extraction is much easier and cheaper. That is why in 1965 the government announces its intention to gradually phase out coal production.

New jobs must be found for the workers who are dismissed: a total of 45,000, not counting the tens of thousands of supply company jobs that will disappear. Despite the government plans to keep employment opportunities up to par, from 1975 onwards the mining region in Limburg is hit by a prolonged economic recession and social decline. Furthermore, the abandoned mines cause new problems: groundwater slowly rises in the highly pol-luted mines, thus becoming contaminated. In addition, the groundwater erodes the former mine shafts, raising the danger of sudden mine subsidence, subsoil sinkholes causing a risk of collapse. In 2011, part of a shopping centre in Heerlen subsides as a result of such a sinkhole.

Gas extraction

By now, the large-scale extraction of natural gas also involves considerable problems. In the province of Groningen, subsoil subsidence regularly causes earthquakes. In recent years, the quakes are increasing in intensity, causing serious damage to homes and other buildings. This creates unrest among local residents, who organise several protest campaigns against the gas extraction. The government intends to turn off the gas entirely by 2022.

New sources of energy

The side effects and consequences of the use of fossil fuels – pollution, earthquakes, but also rising temperatures as a result of CO_2 emissions – will require attention for years to come. Both the European Union and the United Nations have set down agreements on measures to contain such consequences. Converting to new, sustainable forms of energy, such as wind, hydrogen and solar power can be helpful in this respect. The exploration of ways to approach this energy transition constitutes one of the most important issues of our time.

1975-2010

The Caribbean
Far away yet connected

The islands that made up the Netherlands Antilles until 2010 were conquered by the Netherlands in the seventeenth century. They still form part of the Kingdom of the Netherlands. The ties between these islands and the Netherlands are strong but the relationship also experiences tension.

Colonisation

All six islands were conquered by the Netherlands between 1631 and 1648. The SSS Islands – Saba, Sint Eustatius, and Sint Maarten – are located nearly a thousand kilometres north of the ABC Islands – Aruba, Bonaire, and Curaçao. Along with Surinam, they constitute what the Dutch commonly used to refer to as "the West". At this time, these regions are colonial estates in the western hemisphere, where well into the nineteenth century, society is dominated by slavery. Initially, the colonies serve as military bases, trading posts, and plantation colonies. Later on, the oil industry and tourism gain importance.

Decolonisation

The relationship between the Netherlands and these colonies changes radically in the second half of the twentieth century. During World War II, Surinam and the six islands are not occupied by Germany. After the war, they are granted regional autonomy and general suffrage, as so-called "overseas territories". In 1954, the new set-up is anchored in the Charter for the Kingdom of the Netherlands. This is a type of constitution for a trans-atlantic kingdom with autonomous overseas territories.

However, as in other former colonies, the colonial power structures meet with increasing resistance. Residents are dissatisfied with the preponderance of Dutch businesses over the economy of Curaçao, whilst many people on the island live in poverty. In 1969, this leads to strikes, ending in a major popular insurrection. Three hundred Dutch marines are deployed to restore order, which evokes an image of an oppressive colonial power. In order to prevent any further confrontations, the Dutch government opts to give up "the West".

The pursuit of a balance between independence on the one hand and retention of the old connections on the other results in a complex decolonisation process. For example, a large proportion of the population does not support the independence of Surinam in 1975. In the 1970s, some 300,000 Surinamese migrate to the Netherlands. The Netherlands Antilles, as the administrative six island entity is called, do not seek independence; here, the 1954 Charter remains in force for the time being.

Independent

Each island has its own culture and its own interests. Aruba has a thriving economy and for decades has been feeling disadvantaged by the superior political influence of Curaçao. In 1986, Aruba gains a so-called "status aparte", and from 1996 onwards it is an independent constituent country of the Kingdom. However, the search for new forms of government for the Netherlands Antilles is not yet over; eventually, each island decides that a separate relationship with the Netherlands would be better. On 10 October 2010, the Charter is amended, and the Netherlands Antilles officially cease to exist. Now, Curaçao and Sint Maarten are also independent constituent countries within the Kingdom of the Netherlands. They are responsible for their own national administration and legislation. The smaller islands – Bonaire, Sint Eustatius, and Saba – become public bodies of the Netherlands. However, these islands have fewer powers than Dutch municipalities, they are not part of the European Union, and they use the US dollar as their currency.

The Dutch government – which still maintains overall control – is concerned about financial issues in the Caribbean. The islands in their turn are annoyed at the poor provisions and the meddling by the central government in The Hague. Nonetheless, the ties between the Netherlands and these islands remain strong, due to the long, collective history and the many family ties. More than 160,000 Antilleans live in the Netherlands and a growing number of Dutch people settle on the islands. The Netherlands and the Caribbean continue to pursue better mutual collaboration.

1995

Srebrenica

Responsible for peace

Whilst Dutch servicemen are tasked with protecting the Bosnian enclave of Srebrenica, Serbian troops invade and kill nearly all the men. It becomes the worst massacre in post-war European history. The Dutch connection with this event brings the Netherlands great embarrassment and changes its approach to participation in peace missions abroad.

Peace missions

Right from the outset, the Dutch army has participated in United Nations peace operations. Dutch soldiers thus rank among more than a million deployed servicemen from some 120 countries. On behalf of the UN, the troops supervise compliance with peace agreements in several regions. The first mission is launched in 1948, in Israel. A recurrent problem in these operations is the so-called mandate: as peacekeepers, UN soldiers are only allowed to use force in self-defence.

They are given little military leeway to defend and protect civilians.

In 1991, the collapse of the Republic of Yugoslavia is followed by the outbreak of civil war between several federal states. In some states, independence is pursued with great force. In one such state, Bosnia-Herzegovina, the battle between the different groups of the population is particularly fierce. In 1993, the UN Security Council, in its Resolution 819, designates the town of Srebrenica as a "safe area", a so-called enclave. The town is under UN protection, and may no longer be fired upon or besieged by Serbian Bosnians. This enclave harbours a large number of Bosniaks (Bosnian Muslims). The UN sets up a peace force to enforce Resolution 819 in Srebrenica. In 1994, a battalion of Dutch troops, Dutchbat III, is sent to Srebrenica to undertake this task.

Genocide

Dutchbat is but lightly armed and has few means to keep the peace around Srebrenica. In the spring of 1995, Serbian Bosnians start blockading the supply convoys provisioning Dutchbat, which weakens their position even further. In addition, the Serbs attempt to intimidate Dutchbat in all sorts of ways. On 6 July 1995, the Bosnian-Serbian general Ratko Mladić sends his troops towards Srebrenica. Without much resistance, the assailants invade the Bosniak safe haven six days later. Many Bosniak men and boys make a fruitless attempt at escaping.

With assistance from the Dutch soldiers, the Serbs first separate the men and boys who are left behind from the women and children, whereupon they are removed in buses.

They are joined with another group of captured refugees, and shortly thereafter, nearly all these Bosniaks are executed by the Serbs. It is the largest massacre in Europe since the end of World War II. A total of 8,372 names are engraved in the commemorative monument in nearby Potočari.

Responsibility

Once news of the disaster reaches the Netherlands, the question arises as to whether the Dutch soldiers could have done more to protect the enclave from the Serbs. Many Dutch people wonder whether their country has failed on a moral level. The Dutch Institute for War, Holocaust, and Genocide Studies (NIOD) launches a thorough investigation, which goes on for six years. Among other things, the investigation points out the vagueness and the infeasibility of the UN assignment. In fact, the Dutchbat assignment was a mission impossible. When the NIOD report is published in 2002, Prime Minister Wim Kok assumes political responsibility for the disaster in Srebrenica and resigns. Among the Dutch government, the event raises awareness of the complexity of peace missions. From that day on, it ensures that soldiers are sufficiently well armed when being sent on such missions; cases in point are the Dutch missions to Iraq and Afghanistan.

In 2017 and 2019, respectively, the International Criminal Tribunal for the former Yugoslavia convicts the leaders of the Bosnian Serbs, Radovan Karadzić and Ratko Mladić, for their part in the murders. Surviving relatives continue to institute legal proceedings, in the pursuit of answers to questions regarding responsibility and culpability. Srebrenica remains an open wound.

from 1945 onwards

Europe

Joining forces for a peaceful Europe

No more wars that tear Europe apart. That is the main motive
for a collaboration that eventually results in the European Union (EU).
Membership of the EU is supported by a vast majority of the Dutch population.
Others wonder: how far should this collaboration go?

European collaboration

After World War II, European leaders start
exploring ways to prevent a new war.
Several politicians make a case for
European collaboration and integration.
Collaboration is initiated in the field of
strategic resources that are required for
the production of arms. In 1951, France,
Germany, Italy, Belgium, the Netherlands,
and Luxembourg sign the Treaty of Paris, thus
establishing the European Coal and Steel
Community (ECSC). The Treaty stipulates
that the signatories, rather than arranging for
coal and steel production on a national level,
transfer such production to the ECSC.

In 1957, the six member nations sign the Treaty of Rome. This establishes the European Economic Community (EEC): a customs union of the six member nations, guaranteeing free trade in all products. Before long, the EEC initiates a collective agriculture policy, designed by Dutch politician Sicco Mansholt (1908-1995). The policy is aimed at securing food supply and setting up a grant scheme to improve farmers' incomes. European collaboration intensifies and in the years that follow, will extend beyond the economy to culture, education, and the environment.

The European Union
In the early 1990s, the Dutch government is all for the further integration of Europe. Not all the member states are equally enthusiastic. In 1992, during the Dutch presidency of the Council of European Communities, the Treaty of Maastricht is signed, whereby the European Union (EU) is established. The members states intend to intensify their collaboration in the fields of security and justice. And they decide to introduce a common currency, the euro.

From an economic perspective, membership of a large, European free-trade area is of paramount importance to a transit country such as the Netherlands. Other countries also acknowledge the benefits, and the number of EEC and EU member states grows from 6 in 1972 to 28 in 2013.

The EU has a major impact on the lives of its residents. Migration and travel within the Union are easier, whilst goods can be transported anywhere within the EU without border checks. Regulations are harmonised between the countries, which gives the EU increasing control over what the national governments of the member states can and cannot do. For example, Dutch EU Commissioner Neelie Kroes ensures that telecom providers no longer have consumers pay excessively for international telephone calls.

Criticism
The interference from "Brussels" regularly provokes irritation. Most Europeans regard themselves first and foremost as residents of their own national states. Some EU residents start to get the feeling that they are losing control to Europe. They resist further integration; in 2005, for example, the French and the Dutch reject a proposed European "Constitution" through referendums. The euro crisis that breaks out in 2009 puts confidence in the EU under further pressure. The extent to which member states are required to take in refugees is another issue creating profound discord. In 2016, the British vote in favour of "Brexit": leaving the EU. Following a cumbersome process of political negotiations, the exit is finalised in 2020. Despite these developments, most of the 27 remaining member states, including the Netherlands, continue to support the EU. The EU is perceived as important, even indispensable. However, opinions differ widely as to the best way to substantiate European collaboration in the future.

from 1974 onwards

That Orange Feeling

Sport connects

When Dutch athletes excel at the highest level, either individually
or as a team, that Orange Feeling emerges: the streets are decorated
in orange, and people don the most peculiar orange gear.
The Dutch Lion, traditionally a symbol of strength, is omnipresent.

History

From the end of the sixteenth to the end
of the eighteenth centuries, "Orange"
is a political symbol associated with the
Orangists: supporters of the House of Orange
stadtholders. The colour orange comes to be
linked with the identity of the Dutch nation.
During periods of foreign rule, such as the

Napoleonic years and World War II, orange
represents resistance against the foreign
oppressors.

In recent years, the Orange Feeling tends to
play mostly a non-political, connecting role.
It ties in with a growing desire for solidarity

in a society in which differences between people and groups appear to become increasingly wider. The feeling manifests itself, e.g., on occasions such as the Queen's Birthday (from 2013 onwards, the King's Birthday), a national holiday that is first celebrated at the end of the nineteenth century. But also, in times of uncertainty and crisis, "Orange" can give people something to hold on to and a feeling of interconnection.

Sports heroes and heroines

In recent decades, the Orange Feeling is particularly inspired by Dutch athletes participating in important international matches or tournaments. They represent their country, either individually or as a team. During the games, the public sees the Netherlands come into action, concretised by the athlete or the team. This evokes a feeling of national solidarity. The sport of speed skating regularly takes the lead in this respect. An event such as the Frisian ice-skating marathon, which was first held in a competitive format in 1909, combines a group feeling with individual top performances. By the mid-1960s, speed skating events are also the first to boast orange-coloured galleries and orange hats.

Dutch sports history features many sports heroes and sports heroines. Some of them owe their fame not only to their sporting achievements, but also to their wider socio-cultural influence. One such heroine is Fanny Blankers-Koen (1918-2004), who as an athlete becomes a legend when she wins four gold medals during the Olympics of 1948.

This makes her a worldwide role model for sporting women, because she has demonstrated that women are equally capable of competing. Footballer Johan Cruijff (1947-2016), whose extraordinary talent brings the house down at clubs such as Ajax and FC Barcelona, is another athlete to gain world fame. His personality adds to his name: he is straightforward and enriches the Dutch language with Cruijffian one-liners such as *"elk nadeel heb z'n voordeel"* [every disadvantage has its advantage].

Football

Although the Orange Feeling extends to virtually all sports, football still remains the most popular sport in the Netherlands. No wonder then that a genuine Orange Craze may feature especially during international football championships. In 1974, the Orange Feeling in football takes on massive proportions. The Dutch team has made the World Cup finals, but just misses out on the world title after losing to Germany. This is redeemed by winning a European title during the 1988 European Championship. The Dutch team competing in the 1998 World Cup in France is a varicoloured one that reflects the multicultural nature of the Netherlands. In the summer of 2017, the Dutch women win the European Football Championship. In the Netherlands, the finals are watched by a whopping 4.1 million television viewers and the Lionesses are honoured in a grand ceremony in Utrecht. This victory marks the ultimate breakthrough of women's football in the Netherlands. Throughout the ages, Orange has thus reflected the sporting and social changes in the Dutch polder.

Main motifs of the Canon

Era

Up to 3000 BC		Era of Hunters and Farmers
3000 BC–500 AC		Era of Greeks and Romans
500–1000		Era of Monks and Knights
1000–1500		Era of Cities and States
1500–1600		Era of Discoverers and Reformers
1600–1700		Era of Regents and Princes
1700–1800		Era of Wigs and Revolutions
1800–1900		Era of Citizens and Steam Engines
1900–1950		Era of World Wars
1950–Present day		Era of Television and Computer

Motif

Living in a vulnerable delta
The Netherlands: land of water
In a country criss-crossed with major rivers and half situated below
sea level, water largely determines how we live and work. In order
to keep our feet dry, collaboration on water management is
essential here. Even now, the risk of sea or river flooding is never
far away. For how long will we be safe behind our dykes and dams?
The upside is that water also brings riches. Impoldering has
expanded our territory. For centuries, transport by water – from
polder ditch to ocean – has boosted the Netherlands' prime position
as a trading nation. And the remarkable flora and fauna in the
aquatic eco system is garnering increasing attention.

Era	Windows
Up to 3000 BC	Trijntje, Megalithic tombs
3000 BC–500 AC	The Roman *Limes*
500–1000	
1000–1500	The Hanseatic League
1500–1600	
1600–1700	The Beemster
1700–1800	
1800–1900	The first railway
1900–1950	
1950–Present day	The Great Flood, The Port of Rotterdam

Motif

What gives meaning?
Fulfilment and philosophy of life

The quest for meaning and significance is a universal one: "How (or: for whom) do I become a good person?" The various outlooks on life ensuing from this quest help to interconnect and inspire many people. On the other hand, they regularly fill people with an urge to convert others, and in many cases, such different outlooks lead to alienation and conflict between groups. Ideological leaders and institutes are being faced with issues regarding influence and power, and the abuse thereof. How can you form a constructive society with different – religious or other – life principles? Over the course of time, the Netherlands has formulated a range of responses to this question. Authoritative rules, in combination with tolerance and mutual respect, are considered important ingredients for such a society.

Era	Windows	
Up to 3000 BC		Megalithic tombs
3000 BC–500 AC		The Roman *Limes*
500–1000		Willibrord
1000–1500		Hieronymus Bosch, Erasmus
1500–1600		The Revolt
1600–1700		The *States Bible*, Spinoza
1700–1800		*Sara Burgerhart*
1800–1900		The Constitution
1900–1950		Anne Frank
1950–Present day		Srebrenica

Motif

Connecting words and images
Language, art, and culture

For over a thousand years, the Low Countries have formed a continuous cultural area. This is reflected in words and images. Here, the Dutch language is the main vehicle for the mind: speaking and singing, listening and reading, thinking and writing in the same language interconnects us all, even if we challenge one another in terms of content. The literary and visual arts can open up new horizons and cross borders; they record but also influence the spirit of the age. Language and culture are in a constant state of flux; vernacular and slang, folk art and youth culture, old and new media constitute the glue that binds groups together.

Era		Windows
Up to 3000 BC		Trijntje, Megalithic tombs
3000 BC–500 AC		The Roman *Limes*
500–1000		Willibrord
1000–1500		Hebban olla vogala, Hieronymus Bosch, Mary of Burgundy, Erasmus
1500–1600		
1600–1700		The *States Bible*, Rembrandt
1700–1800		*Sara Burgerhart*
1800–1900		*Max Havelaar*, Vincent van Gogh
1900–1950		Anton de Kom, Anne Frank
1950–Present day		Television, The immigrant workers, Annie M.G. Schmidt, *That Orange Feeling*

116

Motif

What do we know?
Knowledge, science, and innovation

Amazing examples of human ingenuity in Dutch history go back a long way: for example, how did the megalith builders manage to lift those heavy boulders off the ground? Every era since has seen an abundance of intellectual, technological, and cultural development. Evidently, this same brainpower can be used in the purview of misuse of power and of destruction. From the eighteenth century onwards, the possibilities for man to bend nature to his will have been gaining momentum. Expansion and computerisation bring prosperity, but also unemployment. Mankind has an ever greater impact on its environment, with an unexpected downside, as is evident by now.

Era		Windows
Up to 3000 BC		Megalithic tombs
3000 BC–500 AC		The Roman *Limes*
500–1000		Charlemagne
1000–1500		Erasmus
1500–1600		
1600–1700		The Beemster, Hugo Grotius, Blaeu's *Atlas Maior*, Christiaan Huygens, Spinoza
1700–1800		Eise Eisinga
1800–1900		The first railway, Aletta Jacobs
1900–1950		
1950–Present day		Television, The Port of Rotterdam

Motif

Who is included?

Social (in)equality

In 1983, the equality before the law of all the residents of the Netherlands was set down in Article 1 of the Dutch Constitution: "Discrimination on the grounds of religion, belief, political opinion, race or sex or on any other grounds whatsoever shall not be permitted." An important Article, because in the course of history, unequal treatment of people and groups turns out to be the rule rather than the exception. People regularly rebel against forms of social inequality and oppression. Sometimes, successfully. In addition to such types of struggle, Dutch social legislation is also underpinned by centuries of brainwork. And still, social inequality is not entirely eradicated.

Era	Windows
Up to 3000 BC	
3000 BC-500 AC	The Roman *Limes*
500-1000	
1000-1500	The Hanseatic League, Mary of Burgundy
1500-1600	The Revolt
1600-1700	Dutch East India Company and Dutch West India Company
1700-1800	Slavery, *Sara Burgerhart*, The Patriots
1800-1900	The Constitution, *Max Havelaar*, The Child Protection Act of Van Houten, Aletta Jacobs
1900-1950	Anton de Kom, Anne Frank, Indonesia
1950-Present day	Marga Klompé, The immigrant workers, Annie M.G. Schmidt, The Caribbean, That Orange Feeling

Motif

Who is governing?
Politics and society

The first outlines of the Netherlands in its present form are already reflected in the principalities of the early Middle Ages. The collective defence of cherished local privileges and prerogatives eventually leads to an independent state. On account of the many different interests and groups, power needs to be shared, which at times results in considerable internal clashes. In the modern era, the Netherlands becomes an administrative entity with increasingly more emphasis on equal rights for all its citizens. The times when independence is jeopardised leave deep wounds. There is a profound desire to safeguard the freedom and peace that have never been a matter of course.

Era		Windows
Up to 3000 BC		
3000 BC–500 AC		The Roman *Limes*
500–1000		Charlemagne
1000–1500		Mary of Burgundy
1500–1600		The Revolt, William of Orange, Johan van Oldenbarnevelt
1600–1700		Michiel de Ruyter
1700–1800		The Patriots
1800–1900		Napoleon Bonaparte, King William I, The Constitution, Aletta Jacobs
1900–1950		World War I, World War II, Indonesia
1950–Present day		Marga Klompé, The Caribbean, Srebrenica, Europe

Motif

Hub of connections
World economy
In this swampy land of rivers, opportunities for agriculture were limited. Consequently, trade and cities start to flourish at an early stage. From the late Middle Ages onwards, the Low Countries develop a modern and innovative economy which turns the region into an important hub of world trade. They are not afraid of engaging in violence and exploitation in this process. Since that time, the area has been attracting large numbers of migrants who help to keep up the economy. The Netherlands has thus been a prosperous country for centuries, although this prosperity is not divided equally. The economy benefits from open borders; however, its extreme dependence on such open borders renders it vulnerable.

Era	Windows
Up to 3000 BC	
3000 BC-500 AC	The Roman *Limes*
500-1000	Charlemagne
1000-1500	The Hanseatic League
1500-1600	
1600-1700	Dutch East India Company and Dutch West India Company, Blaeu's *Atlas Maior*, Michiel de Ruyter
1700-1800	Slavery
1800-1900	The first railway
1900-1950	
1950-Present day	Television, The Port of Rotterdam, The immigrant workers, Coal and gas, Europe